Award-winning writer, ~~journalist, broadcaster and social~~
activist, **Leslie Kenton** i~~~~
ism, television and vid~~~~

world. She is the autho~~~~
health including *The N*~~~~
The New Joy of Beauty, T~~~~
– Natural Menopause R~~~~
major shifts in the way doctors and women are approaching
the treatment of PMS, osteoporosis and menopausal problems.

Leslie's books have been translated into several foreign
languages and her journalism has appeared in every national newspaper in Britain and many abroad. She was also
Health and Beauty Editor for *Harpers & Queen* for 14 years.
Her network television series include *Raw Energy*, a cookery
series for Thames, and *Ageless Ageing* for HTV which she
conceived, wrote and presented herself. She has also made
a series of short films on health for the BBC.

Leslie lectures throughout the world continually striving
to bring to light natural methods of enhancing health and
good looks that enable people to gain more control over
their own lives, achieve a high degree of autonomy, and
make better use of their personal creativity. She has always
insisted that real health comes from within and the only
true 'guru' is the individual human soul. The techniques,
tools and information about enhancing health and good
looks which she shares with her viewers and readers are
merely the tools for helping us to realize our own potential
for energy, health and personal freedom and for improving
our lives so we can give more to our families, our communi-
ties and the planet itself.

The Leslie Kenton approach to health is a unique
combination of self-care based on the long tradition of
nature cure – from hydrotherapy and high raw diets to
consciousness-altering mind games – and cutting-edge
scientific findings about how to alter brain chemistry to
shift behaviour and reverse the ageing process . . . *naturally*.

Her high public profile and her consistent ability to practise what she preaches has brought her much admiration as
have her vibrant personality and youthful good looks. Leslie
is the daughter of American jass musician Stan Kenton.

10 STEPS TO ENERGY

Leslie Kenton

VERMILION
LONDON

**For
Claire Bowles
may her energy be endless
and her joy**

3 5 7 9 10 8 6 4

Text copyright © Leslie Kenton 1997, 1998

The right of Leslie Kenton to be identified as the author of this book
has been asserted by her in accordance with the Copyright, Designs
and Patents Act, 1988.

First published in the United Kingdom in 1997 by Ebury Press

This edition first published in the United Kingdom in 1998 by Vermilion

an imprint of Ebury Press
Random House
20 Vauxhall Bridge Road
London SW1V 2SA

Random House Australia (Pty) Limited
20 Alfred Street, Milsons Point, Sydney,
New South Wales 2061, Australia

Random House New Zealand Limited
18 Poland Road, Glenfield,
Auckland 10, New Zealand

Random House South Africa (Pty) Limited
PO Box 337, Bergvlei, South Africa

Random House Canada
1265 Aerowood Drive, Mississauga,
Ontario L4W 1B9, Canada

Random House UK Limited Reg. No. 954009

A CIP catalogue record for this book is available
from the British Library.

0 09 181686 6

Printed and bound in Norway by
AIT Trondheim AS

Papers used by Ebury Press are natural recyclable products made
from wood grown in sustainable forests.

Contents

	Author's Note	6
Step One	**Claim Your Right to Energy**	7
Step Two	**Take Stock**	18
Step Three	**Collar the Energy Thieves**	28
Step Four	**Face the Body Snatchers**	49
Step Five	**Clear Out the Junk**	68
Step Six	**Bite into Energy**	80
Step Seven	**Fuel Up from Nature**	102
Step Eight	**Charge Your Batteries**	114
Step Nine	**Grin and Bear It**	128
Step Ten	**Dare to Be You**	137
	Resources	148
	Further Reading	154
	Index	157

Author's Note

The material in this book is intended for information purposes only. None of the suggestions or information is meant in any way to be prescriptive. Any attempt to treat a medical condition should always come under the direction of a competent physician – and neither the publisher nor I can accept responsibility for injuries or illness arising out of a failure by a reader to take medical advice. I am only a reporter. I also have a profound interest in helping myself and others to maximize our potential for positive health which includes being able to live at a high level of energy, intelligence and creativity. For all three are expressions of harmony within a living organic system.

I want to make it clear that I have no commercial interest in any product, treatment or organization mentioned in this book. However, I have long sought to learn more about whatever can help us to live well and joyfully, for it is my belief that the more each one of us is able to re-establish harmony within ourselves and with our environment, the better equipped we shall be to wrestle with the challenges now facing our planet.

Step One
Claim Your Right to Energy

All of us have a lot more potential energy than we ever access. For most of us our natural energy lies buried deep in a sluggish body burdened with excessive toxicity or a psyche wrestling with frustration or disappointment. We may even have the sense that we are not really living the life we want to live. And we feel powerless to change things. Yet they *can* be changed. Each one of us can learn to release our energy potential and live it out. It is not even that hard to do once you decide it is energy you want.

This book is about how to break through the barriers by making changes in how you think, eat and live that will help you turn potential energy into lasting vitality. It looks carefully at certain underlying conditions such as food allergies, yeast overgrowths and environmental pollutants which can undermine our natural energy rights. It helps you identify the presence of any of the big energy drainers in your life and then suggests how you can take steps to clear them. In this book you will also find loads of tricks and treatments to help you build steady energy week after week and year after year, as well as suggestions about how to summon extra energy temporarily when you most need it. Finally, this book is designed to help you discover for yourself the greatest energy secret of all: that living a high-energy life is ultimately about learning to listen to the whispers of your own soul and to live out the truth of who you really *are* and what you really *value*.

Power When You Need It

Everyone has experienced the ability to summon up energy almost magically when it is most needed to cope with particularly demanding situations – the appearance of a 'second wind'. It happens when you have been up all night nursing a sick child and thought you couldn't possibly drag up another ounce of strength. It happens when all-encompassing fatigue somehow disappears into thin air with the unexpected arrival of a much-loved friend you haven't seen for years; and when an athlete discovers he can call forth extra strength on the last lap of a long race. In these circumstances we can summon energy because, in our psyche, we ask for it – right now – to do what we want passionately to do.

Feeling passionate about anything releases potential energy, both immediately where it is needed, and also long-term, where we need energy to carry out some task we are deeply committed to, or do something we love. And living with energy has a lot to do with living with passion.

The more passionately you live your life the more energy you will generate. Do what you love, love what you do and be honest about it. Much of our energy comes from *within*.

Lifestyle Energy Factors

But this is only half of the energy picture. The amount of vitality available to you day by day to live your life also comes from *external* forces – from the way you eat, exercise, deal with stress and look after your body, as well as how skilful you become at listening to its needs and its promptings. For most of us this doesn't happen automatically, nor does a high energy way of life. We have to learn what creates more energy in our lives and also learn to be wary of all the things which can impede it.

Toxicity in your body is just one of the negative forces. The build-up of waste products in the cells restricts metabolic processes and depletes us of energy both bio-chemically – so we become more prone to illness and premature ageing – and in terms of overall stamina and vitality – or how energetic we *feel* subjectively. Internal pollution can also result in a great variety of unwanted conditions – from cellulite to poor skin, anxiety and degenerative conditions such as arthritis, obesity and cancer. In the highly polluted environment in which most of us live our bodies tend to build up more waste than they are able to eliminate efficiently. Such a build-up suppresses our energy. It needs to be eliminated and prevented in the future. To maximize vitality you also need to learn to manage your energies when they need managing – how to get down when you become strung up, how to stimulate vitality when it is low and how to create stamina and sustained power that acts as a founda-tion of energy that you can always call on when you need it. We will take a good look at how to do all of this.

Living High

It may surprise you, but the first step towards a high-energy life is not a physical one, but is a change in how you think. It starts when you begin to visualize what living with sustained energy feels like.

This can be hard to do when you feel chronically fatigued, depressed and discouraged. 'Will my life ever get better?' we ask ourselves. I know. I lived for many years with chronic fatigue and depression – for which doctors could find no apparent cause. I have experi-enced the struggle and sense of hopelessness one can feel. In fact in a very real way those years helped shape the values of my life and set me on the road to learning, writing, and broadcasting on health. What happened was that because nobody seemed able to help me I began to look for my own answers. What I learned did help me and I went on to share it with others through books, tele-vision, videos and workshops.

Shift Your Perspective

Our culture teaches us that all phenomena in the Universe, even life itself, are no more than a complex, yet explicable, series of chemical and physical reactions devoid of any unseen organizing principle. Such a world view has its limitations. We tend to favour the notion that man's task is to harness nature for his own ends – and then are appalled at the results.

This materialistic perspective has contributed to a sense of human alienation expressed in our art, literature, and in destructive social behaviour. It is also responsible in no small part for our flagging energy. For we often tend to dissipate ourselves trying to fulfil all sorts of roles and follow all sorts of rules that we unthinkingly impose on ourselves.

We are told that we need to go to the gym to give us more energy, and also that we need to eat the latest 'healthy' margarine promoted by the food industry. We are urged to do our jobs well, no matter what distractions or restrictions we may have, and we feel we need to keep going to meet all our deadlines however much our bodies may be telling us we need to stop and rest. We have also been conditioned by a culture that affirms the value of altruism and insists that one should forget oneself in constant service and self-sacrifice to others.

If you are serious about wanting more energy you need to make a shift in how you think about yourself and your life. Gaining more energy is not simply a case of changing a few seemingly unrelated things in your life. It is a change in attitude and lifestyle that follows a simple yet powerful personal choice – the choice to support your body and mind in the best possible ways. Once you have chosen, then you can begin to make positive changes towards creating more energy. As you do you will also find more and more positive changes taking place as greater access to energy in one area of your life allows you to deal more clearly with fatigue in another.

Total Involvement

One factor which has a powerful influence on how much energy you have is not your physical strength, or what you had for lunch, nor even how much sleep you got last night, but rather whether or not you are totally involved at any particular moment in what you are doing – physically, mentally, and emotionally. To be able to live energetically what you are doing has to have value to you. It has in some way to feed your soul or satisfy some longing or value or goal for you. Biologists, sports experts, and psychologists have recently studied the phenomenon of energy or vitality and tried to distinguish between the traits of those people with high energy levels and the rest of us. They have discovered that, whether looking at sportsmen, executives, artists, or craftsmen, those with high energy all have one thing in common: total involvement.

A few lucky people – often those who are vitally interested in their work or hobbies – find total involvement comes naturally. For the rest of us it has to be learned. We have to train ourselves in much the same way as students of disciplines such as Aikido, Japanese sword training, or Tai Chi do – slowly and systematically.

In Western society it is sadly rare to find people who function as a whole. Most of us tend to do whatever we are doing with half our thoughts on what we are *going* to do when we have finished, or thinking about what we *should* have done yesterday but didn't. Such distractions not only make the task in hand seem long and tedious, they also divide our concentration, with the result that energy is dissipated. For more energy, make a commitment to becoming deeply involved in the process of energy creation in your life. The opposite is true too. Where living the 'right' way for *you* breeds more energy, living in a way that ignores your basic values will have you fighting yourself and the world around you and continually drain your vitality.

11

The Energy-Drainer Scenario

I'll show you what I mean. A woman is in a job which she hates. She feels unmotivated and resentful (*inner energy-drainer*). After work she goes out to drink (*alcohol-addiction energy-drainer*). Sometimes she drinks too much and this creates friction with her husband (*relationship energy-drainer*). She feels bad about herself as a result of arguing (*emotional energy-drainer*). Her poor self-image leads her not to care for herself (*poor self-esteem energy-drainer*). She eats badly (*biochemical energy-drainer*). She feels worse and suffers depression. Nothing in her life seems to work and she has nothing to look forward to . . .

You can see the pattern. She is stuck in a rut. The energy-drainers have stolen her ability to see the wood for the trees and she can only see everything in the worst light. Now let's look at the flip side. Energy-enhancers tend to attract other energy-enhancers, giving you back control of your life. Compare the following situation with the previous sketch.

The Energy-Enhancer Scenario

A woman is in a job which she hates. She discovers an inspiring exercise class (*physical energy-enhancer*). The class makes her feel good about herself and inspires her to eat better (*biochemical energy-enhancer*). She loses a few pounds, feels better in her body and begins to dress in a more flattering way (*self-esteem energy-enhancer*). She meets some new friends whose company she really enjoys (*relationship energy-enhancer*). As her self-esteem increases, the people she works with begin to appreciate her more. Her job becomes more enjoyable (*emotional energy-enhancer*). She feels excited about her life and confident about looking for a new job, something she will really love.

Being able to call on your energy potentials depends on how well you nourish yourself – physically, emotionally and spiritually – day by day. This means developing a lifestyle which incorporates exercise, good food, restorative sleep and the myriad of other possible factors – from hydrotherapy to supernutrients – that help support your own brand of vitality at peak efficiency.

Your Body as Energy

When creating such a lifestyle there is one simple but essential thing to remember: your body *is* energy. What your body most certainly is *not* (although at the worst of times it can feel a lot like it) is some dense physical object you have to bolster up or beat into submission so it can keep going.

Practically everything that is written about the body in terms of exercise, nutrition, and health-supporting treatments is hung up on the outdated mechanical world view which ignores this fundamental truth. The standard advice about health and good looks leaves out the fact that as a living organism every physical and chemical change that takes place in your body is really a *secondary* effect of some *primary* energy change.

Learning a little about what influences your body as a unified energetic system and beginning to think of it in this way will help you understand how powerful an effect your thinking has on how much energy you have. It will also enable you to call on simple yet incredibly potent energy-enhancing, energy-altering and energy-supporting practices which can make everything in your life a lot easier.

Take One Rat – Dead or Alive

More than sixty years ago, a brilliant scientist, Albert Szent-Györgyi, used to ask a simple question at dinner parties: 'What is the difference between a living rat and a dead one?' According to the laws of classical chemistry and physics based on the old world view there is no fundamental difference. Yet as any fool can see this

13

is rubbish. Szent-Györgyi's own reply was simple yet revolutionary – 'Some kind of electricity.'

Szent-Györgyi, who won two Nobel prizes for his work, had years earlier observed that the molecular structure of a living cell somehow acts as a semiconductor for electromagnetic or magnetic energy. Semiconduction takes place only in materials which have a highly ordered structure, such as crystals, in which the atoms are arranged in neat geometrical lattices. This enables electrons to move with ease from the orbit of one molecule to another. When it comes to health it is the ease with which such electron transfer takes place that largely determines the experience of *aliveness*, both in an individual cell and in the body as a whole. But it was not until an outstanding American orthopaedic surgeon named Robert O. Becker came along that a real understanding of the energy control system in the human body began to be understood.

Energy Control Starts Here

Becker postulated that an analogue-coded electronic information system exists in the body which carries energetic information to regulate cell division and healing and to support life processes. This system is likely to be the interface by which our thoughts are able to induce physical and biochemical changes in our bodies (how spiritual healing works, for instance, as well as the process of creative visualization that is used for healing and for improving sports performance).

Putting his theory into practice with animal studies, Becker discovered that such a system does indeed exist. It has regulating, self-organizing and self-repairing properties based on semiconductivity, and it is strongly influenced for good or ill by magnetic and electromagnetic fields. Becker went on to explore the way in which the 'information' from magnetic and electromagnetic fields affect human beings for good or ill and to caution that many electromagnetic influences in day-to-day life – from electric blankets to microwaves – can be highly detrimental to health. This may all sound high-falutin' and super-scientific, but it is important. Once you get the sense of your body as energy you can make sense of learning how to support it with tools such as exercise, how you eat, and how you think. And once you get a sense of how powerfully emotions, such as laughter and grief, raise and lower your vitality, you can begin to break through the feeling of separation from your body which makes us prey to self-neglect and feelings of inade-quacy and powerlessness. So the first step in putting more energy in your body and your life is simply to shift your perspective. Let's look at what comes next.

Ready, Steady, Go

There are ten steps to making the most of energy – ten ways in which you can alter your lifestyle to support your mind and your body. Each step works synergistically to support the others. Once you make the decision to change one small part of your life, you will automatically feel empowered to do something about the rest.

STEP ONE:
Decide You Have a Right to Energy

Our mind, emotions and values are elaborately inter-woven with the functions of our body via nerve pathways and chemical messengers such as *endorphins*, *intestinal peptides* and *hormones*. It is little wonder that the levels of energy you experience depend on how you think about yourself. The physical changes that you may need to make – with exercise, diet, and relaxation – are depen-dent on your acknowledging that who you are and what you want REALLY MATTERS. The first step to energy asks that you do two things: firstly, shift your perspective so you no longer see your body as external to yourself, to be pushed, prodded or driven – but rather as the

15

physical and energetic manifestation of who you are. Secondly, decide you matter – that you have a right to energy and are willing to make the self-explorations and learn the stuff you need to learn in order to develop it.

STEP TWO:
Check Out Where You Are Now

When embarking on the energy journey it is important to know where you are as you begin. This means taking stock of how you feel, how you think, what you want and what you think may be stopping you.

STEP THREE:
Get Smart About the Energy Thieves – And Counter Them

We live in a world where all sorts of influences tend to drain us of energy – from heavy metals and chemical toxicity in our air and foods to drugs and changes in the weather. So do negative emotions like anxiety and depression. It is time to become aware of which of these 'energy thieves' may be operating in your life and begin taking action to counter them.

STEP FOUR:
Defeat Biochemical Energy-Drainers

If your metabolic processes are out of whack so is your energy. Chronic low blood sugar, hypothyroidism, a proliferation of Candida albicans in the system, food allergies and anaemia all undermine energy. Find out if they are present in your body and take steps to clear them.

STEP FIVE:
Detoxify Your Body

Having taken stock and dealt with energy thieves and drainers, from now on the journey towards energy is all about taking action. And the first action to take is to clear out the rubbish to release potential energy into your life.

STEP SIX:
Let Food Do It
How you eat, how much you eat, what you eat, and when you eat it all strongly influence your energy levels both immediately and long term. Learn the secrets of energy eating and begin to put them into practice.

STEP SEVEN:
Get Help from Nature
Special plants, fungi, grasses and herbs can in one way or another enhance life energies and heighten vitality. Make friends with them – you will be glad that you have.

STEP EIGHT:
Balance Your Energy Act
Maintaining high energy demands that we learn the arts of energetic balance – moving the body, playing with the breath, learning to get down when you are up, and up when you are down. It is all part of good energy management and an important step to lasting energy.

STEP NINE:
Start Laughing
Joyful play and learning to 'follow your bliss' are powerful energy-makers and a lot of fun. You will have learned most of the serious stuff; now is the time to let go and start living with energy.

STEP TEN:
Chart Your Energy Future
Pull it all together and make a life plan which includes being yourself, setting goals, making the most of daily energy practices, monitoring your energy progress and sketching your energy future. This is the beginning of the rest of your life. Enjoy it.

Going for energy means embarking on an energy journey that will lead you in and out of biochemistry, self-awareness, resolution and experiment towards the development of new ways of thinking and living life. It can be a lot of fun. Let's do it.

Take Stock

Congratulations, you have already taken the first step towards energy – you have made up your mind to learn what needs to be learned and to go for it. Soon you can begin to change your lifestyle for the better. In the chapters that follow you will find out about energy habits, tricks, tips and balancers to help steer you through the maze of energy thieves we encounter in our daily lives. But before you can make the best use of them you need to take the second step towards high energy: to find out where you are *right now* on the energy scale. It's time to take stock.

Make a Workbook

A workbook, or diary (for your eyes only), is a great tool for moving your life into high gear. Your workbook will become a real friend and companion on your energy journey. It is also a place where you can share all your hopes, fears, triumphs and disappointments. This is important when building energy. Your workbook will be your own personal monitor of how well you are proceeding along your Ten Steps To Energy. So find a notebook that you like the look of, which has good quality paper that is nice to write on, and a pen you enjoy writing with.

Self-Monitoring Starts Here

Self-monitoring is vital, both objectively – how much weight you are losing, how much further you can run – and subjectively in how you feel about yourself and your life.

First let's get a good idea of where you are now in relation to energy potential. Begin by writing in your workbook the answers to the following questions. Answer them as honestly, as fully, and as accurately as you can. (If you don't record your answers, if you only answer verbally, you won't get nearly as much from the experience.) What works best is black and white evidence made today which you can come back to and compare with your answers to the same questions a few weeks down the road. Your energy workbook will also help you, day to day and week to week, see more clearly what action you need to take.

1. How well do you sleep? Do you need a lot of sleep or are you content with six or seven hours a night? Do you dream vividly? Do your dreams seem of interest to you and do they have meaning? Or do you simply 'crash out' when you hit the bed each night?

2. How do you feel in the morning? Clear-headed and cheerful? Looking forward to the day ahead, no matter what it brings? Or are you still fatigued after a night's sleep? Would you prefer to stay in bed for the rest of the morning if you could?

3. How are your energy levels throughout the day? Do you feel you need a cup of coffee to keep going? Do you have a tendency to 'wear out' in the middle of the morning or afternoon? Are you so bouncy after a day's work that you can look forward to going out in the evening?

4. How much fun do you have? Do you find yourself laughing easily at little things? Are you able to enjoy yourself without heavy doses of alcohol and being entertained all the time? Do you enjoy your work as much as your play?

5. How do you feel about your life? Is it something you endure or something you feel excited about? How about when you look towards the future? Would you trade places with anybody else in the world?

Depth Sounding

You have probably had the experience of waking up with the sense that the whole world is against you, and the events of the day confirm your opinion. The opposite is also true. When you feel good about yourself it can seem as though you are living a charmed life where everything (or just about everything) falls into place with ease. You find a parking space, the bank stops losing your deposits, everyone seems to remember your birthday.

Despite the way our culture tends to separate body and mind, your body is nothing less than your soul incarnate. Like opposite ends of the continuum, mind and body play an equal part in energy generation. To build energy that lasts and lasts we need to address the outer and inner issues simultaneously. Take a look at the next set of questions and answer them in your workbook. Really pour out what you *feel*. There are no right or wrong answers – just *your* answers. Nobody is ever going to read this except you. If some of your answers seem negative, great. At least you know where your starting point is. It is virtually impossible to bring about real transformation in your life without being very honest about what is happening right now. Only when we establish this kind of base awareness do we open the door to real change. Here we go:

Energy Factors – Self-Check List

Answer the following questions honestly. I have given you some examples as a guide but write whatever comes to mind first. Just let rip.

1. **What are your first thoughts on waking?**
   ● I am confused.
   ● I just want to go back to sleep.
   ● I am excited about the day ahead.
   ● I am anxious/depressed.
   ● Other?

2. **When you look in the mirror what do you feel?**
   - I fret over my wrinkles/grey hair/blemishes and feel down about myself.
   - I feel happy with the way I look – imperfections and all.
   - I don't think I matter much.
   - Other?

3. **When confronted with a difficult task at home or at work what do you think?**
   - What a pain, maybe if I avoid it someone else will do it.
   - Here's a challenge, something to really get my teeth into.
   - I feel overwhelmed but determined.
   - Other?

4. **When looking forward to a romantic evening what do you do?**
   - I create a scenario of doom in case things don't work out – that way I won't be disappointed.
   - I enjoy imagining how wonderful the evening is going to be.
   - I live in the moment and just let the chips fall as they may.
   - Other?

5. **When you have an argument with your partner what do you think?**
   - This is typical, he/she doesn't understand me.
   - There must be something wrong with *me*.
   - How do we build a bridge back to each other?
   - Other?

6. **When you get a cold what do you think?**
   - Just my luck. I always catch a cold at the worst possible times.
   - I must be run down. What can I do to improve my overall health?
   - I'll take a lot of cold remedies and aspirin and just forget it.
   - Other?

7. **When you are paid a compliment what do you do?**
   - I dismiss it and try to work out what they want out of me.
   - I accept graciously and thank them for their kindness.
   - Feel embarrassed and that they don't mean it.
   - Other?

8. **What do you think about your job?**
   - I hate it. I'm overworked and underpaid, but I have to do it, there is so much unemployment and where am I going to find another one?
   - I enjoy my work. It gives me a chance to do something I am good at, and get financially rewarded for doing it.
   - It isn't what I want ultimately but I am moving towards changing it.
   - Other?

9. **When you look back on your past what do you think?**
   - I feel resentful about the opportunities I missed and regret many of the things I have and haven't done.
   - I am happy that the decisions I have made – good and bad – have brought me to this point. If I went back I wouldn't change anything.
   - I don't think much about my past, I'm more concerned with now.
   - Other?

10. **On what do you feel your future happiness depends?**
    - Finding the right relationship, the right job, earning lots of money, winning the lottery, and hoping not too much goes wrong.
    - Me living the way I want to live without compromise and letting my life unfold in optimistic anticipation.
    - Luck.
    - Other?

Secrets of Truth Telling

When it comes to having lots of energy the big secret is simple: TELL THE TRUTH. This may sound trivial or even beside the point. Yet being able to *be* whomever you are, *say* whatever you think and *feel* without guilt, recrimination or justification whatever you feel breaks down all the energy barriers in your life. It also brings a sense of freedom that we have as children but lose when we take on the trappings and complexities of adulthood.

As we grow up we learn to change ourselves or mask what we really want or think because we fear we are not acceptable. Yet pretence of any kind – either to oneself or to others – drains natural energy fast. There is a way of learning to live in relative peace and harmony with people around you and still be who you really are. It takes time, of course, for each of us to learn how, and it asks that you affirm not only that you matter but also that each and every other being on the planet matters and has an equal right to be what they are and live true to themselves.

Energy from the Source

At the core of each of us sleeps our soul – that part that makes us utterly unique and has encoded within it our goals, characteristics and potentials – both physical and spiritual – all these traits and powers we are ultimately on the earth in order to realize. The more we are aware of the nature of our *soul energy*, of its real intentions and of what brings us joy at the deepest levels, the easier it becomes to live out who we are – to tell our truth. Once truth begins to be told, it becomes easier to clear out unfulfilling behaviour patterns, relationships, and ways of living which drain our life energies and do not feed our soul. As we are able to identify and lift off these things, we release the most enormous surge of creative energy. Think of how you feel when you are doing something you love – energy just seems to pour forth. Compare this to the way you feel when you lie, compromise, and do your duty. Which would you rather experience?

Believe it or not, it *is* possible with each passing month – regardless of the situation, relationship, job or physical condition you find yourself in at the moment – to move closer and closer to living from your core, feeding your soul, expanding your creativity and empowering others to do the same. As you do this, those parts of your life that are not now working as well as you would like them to begin to change for the better. As they do so, your energy levels just build and build. The inner path towards energy requires that each of us learn to listen to what I call the whispers of the soul – and then slowly but surely start putting what they tell us into practice.

Soul Secrets

Most of us have never learned how to do this. Instead we have been taught *not* to listen to our inner voice. We have been filled with all sorts of stuff by our parents, our educational system, our bosses, our spouses and the media which teaches us *not* to trust ourselves but rather to live our lives according to external 'rules'. These rules may be homilies like 'always think of others first', 'you must not succeed or somebody might be jealous', 'you must not do that – so-and-so wouldn't like it'. Or they can come from advertisements that would have us believe that what we *are* is not good enough, and that we need a new car, job, image, body, just in order to be OK.

The kind of internal dialogue which goes through our minds as we are continually bombarded in this way drains our energies. It also creates a lot of 'static' which obscures the softer voices from our core – soul whispers about things like what we really value, what we want or what we are.

It takes a little practice to develop the skill of listening to your inner voice. Strangely, the first whispers you hear may make no sense at all. For instance for many years I longed for a pair of red shoes but I never bought them. I guess it seemed selfish and trivial to me when I was earning a living to support four children. But also (and I didn't realize this until much later) red shoes seemed very *dangerous* to me – the kind of things a gypsy might wear to dance on the table – something not allowed (I felt) in the life of a 'responsible' woman like me. Well, one day I decided to go for it and buy a pair.

A Passion for Red Shoes

It was great. This simple, trivial act made me feel freer and lighter. Whenever I wore the shoes I found myself having a lot of fun. They seemed to release a hidden side to my character which had been lurking beneath my rather conventional, 'proper' personality. With it came lots of creative, playful energy.

What I discovered from heeding the call to own a pair of red shoes was something far more important than the shoes themselves. I found out that when you begin to listen to inner whispers about relatively *trivial* things, your inner voice gradually, yet inexorably, gets louder. Before long you are hearing the answers to much more important questions and getting much more vital information about your health, your values, your goals, and your life. And as soul whispers grow louder and clearer, your experience of meaning in your life grows with them. So does your experience of energy.

Living with quantum energy asks that we build a bridge between the inner and outer parts of our life so that less of our potential for life energy gets blocked, suppressed, or dissipated. This depends on listening to the whispers, becoming more aware of how you want to live, eat, exercise and live your life, and putting into practice what you hear, bit by bit, to see what works for you and what doesn't.

Four Keys to Your Soul

Let's turn back to your workbook. This powerful energy-expanding process is an ongoing one. Let it begin by exploring your answers to four simple questions in your workbook.

Ask yourself the questions below one at a time. Then, letting your mind roam free, write down whatever comes to you. You may feel that the answer to one demands reams of words while the answer to another is very short. Explore each question fully before going on to the next. The questions are:

1. Who am I?

This does not mean your name and where you come from but rather what comes to your mind when the question is asked. How do you see yourself? What are you like?

2. What do I want?

This should include everything you feel you want or anything you secretly dream of, from the tiniest thing such as, 'I want to take up tapestry,' or 'I have always wanted to ride a motorcycle' to huge desires you may never have dared to voice: 'I want to go off to Africa to help people dig wells,' 'I want to look and feel 15 years younger,' or 'I want to write a novel.' It doesn't matter, just write it down.

3. What do I *think* is stopping me?

Make a note of any circumstance, person, place, thing, thought or feeling that you feel stands in your way.

4. Where am I right now in relation to what I want?

To create what you want in your life – from greater self-esteem to your dream home – you need two things. First, you need as clear a vision as possible of what it is you are seeking, and secondly, you need to be certain of where you are right now in relation to that vision. The greater your desire to achieve a goal and the clearer you can be about where you are in relation to that goal, the easier the achievement of that goal becomes.

These four questions, by the way, are not the kind of thing that there are pat answers to. The answers to your questions are going to change as you change. As you move through Ten Steps To Energy refer back to them periodically. See how these answers alter and develop as your soul-awareness grows.

The process of energy exploration is enormously dynamic. Sometimes it is a lot of fun and sometimes it can be very demanding. In fact the road to energy has certain common principles which we will be looking at in the chapters that follow, but remember that the individual journey each of us takes along the road is unique.

Step Three
Collar the Energy Thieves

Our world is full of energy thieves. Excessive noise, environmental poisons and allergy-provoking chemicals in our air, water and food: all these things can drain us of energy. Eating junk foods is another big-time energy thief. Even changes in the weather can drain our energy. So does heavy emotional stress from anxiety, resentment or depression. Such delinquent influences also lower your immunity, make you vulnerable to catching colds and 'flu and susceptible to premature ageing and the development of degenerative conditions. For lasting high energy the energy thieves in your life need to be cornered, collared and dealt a fatal blow.

Scan Your Environment

A major issue in energy-making is to keep your body clean – inside and out. This way you help protect yourself from the damage which toxic substances in our environment can cause. Your body stores much of the damaging waste it picks up in your tissues – particularly in fat cells. Any kind of stored waste or toxicity suppresses vitality and immunity. Only spring-cleaning your body from inside can release it (see Step 5, Clear Out the Junk). A properly functioning immune system is dependent on your body's ability to clear itself of the destructive chemicals we encounter every day in our food, our air, our water – even in the plastics in which we store or microwave our foods. Here are just a few of the energy-stealing environmental hazards the body has to overcome:

- antibiotics
- cleaning solvents
- cadmium and lead in cigarette smoke
- mercury from fillings in teeth
- aluminium from anti-perspirants, pots and pans and antacids
- lead solder from canned foods
- oestrogens from oral contraceptives and HRT
- anabolic steroids
- non-steroid anti-inflammatory drugs
- contaminated foods
- solvents like formaldehyde, acetone and toluene
- pesticides and herbicides: DDT, DDB, dioxins and halogenates like PCB and PCP which act as oestrogen mimics and screw up our reproductive systems

Heavy Work for Your Liver

The organ at the centre of clearing the body of environmental pollutants is the liver. When your liver is working well and is not overburdened with potentially destructive elements, your body remains clean, your immune system is free to function well, and your energy levels can soar. When the liver is not working well neither is the immune system. The liver, which manufactures important biochemical factors that are needed by the immune system, helps produce lymph and plays an important part in clearing the blood of cellular rubbish, yeasts, bacteria, and other negative micro-organisms. Good liver function is central to an experience of high energy. Damage to the liver and poor liver function is invariably present when someone has Chronic Fatigue Syndrome or Epstein Barr virus, as it is when there is an overgrowth of Candida albicans. When your liver is functioning poorly all sorts of problems show up – for many of which the average doctor has no explanation and no safe effective treatment. These can include depression, confusion, constant fatigue, numbness in hands and feet, headaches, aches and pains, sweating and impaired function of the nervous system.

As any good practitioner of natural medicine will tell you, at the core of every person with chronic low energy is an over-taxed, under-functioning liver. Experts often refer to it as a *sluggish liver* or a *congested liver*. Unfortunately a sluggish or congested liver can be tough to identify using standard medical tests. Often physical damage to the liver has occurred before poor functioning of the liver shows up in these tests. Nutritionally orientated doctors prefer therefore to use other tests which establish how quickly your liver clears a specific substance and can therefore determine how well your liver really is working long before serious damage has taken place. If you are chronically tired, here's how you can take steps to protect your body from pollutants as much as possible and give your liver some extra support to do its job well:

Environmental Protection and Liver Support

- If you use paints or solvents always wear a mask.
- If you smoke, stop; if others around you do, stay away from them.
- Always choose biodegradable cleaning products and forget the chlorine bleaches. Avoid as many environmental pollutants as possible.
- Don't cook foods in plastic containers in a microwave.
- Explore having the amalgam fillings in your mouth replaced with safer alternatives.
- Stay away from all drugs – prescription and otherwise – unless they are absolutely necessary.
- Exercise moderately but regularly – long walks are a great way to energize liver functions.
- Grow your own foods in the garden organically and go on a 2-day fresh juice fast or fruit fast (see Step 5, Clear Out the Junk) or a 10-day high raw regime every three months (see Resources).
- Switch to High Energy Eating for 3 to 6 months (see Step 6, Bite into Energy) – even better, forever.

Look After Your Liver

Without a top-notch liver lasting energy will always elude you. Make a note in your workbook today if you feel your liver is struggling. Write out exactly how you feel. You will be able to come back and compare what you have written with how different you feel six weeks into your energy journey.

Natural Liver Support

- **take anti-oxidant nutrients:** a good multi-vitamin supplement taken for several weeks or months can help the liver handle the elimination of toxicity and heavy metals (see Resources, page 148).

- **try milk thistle:** this plant (*Silybum marianum*) is rich in bioflavinoid compounds with powerful protective and anti-oxidant properties – many times more powerful than vitamin C and vitamin E. A supplement of clean milk thistle enhances detoxification, increases the liver's capacity to neutralize and detoxify harmful chemicals and heavy metals and protects the body's natural anti-oxidant enzymes from damage. Nutritionally orientated doctors recommend between 80 and 200mg of milk thistle three times a day (see Resources, page 151 for a good clean supply).

- **use lipotrophic agents:** compounds such as choline, betaine, l-methionine, and l-cysteine are known as lipotrophic agents – that is, they help promote the flow of bile and the breakdown of fats in the body. Lipotrophics increase the levels of a couple of important liver elements – S-adenosylmethionine (SAM) and glutathione – a super detoxifier and protector from free radical damage. They are used to treat lots of liver disorders – from cirrhosis and chemically caused liver damage to hepatitis – naturally (see Resources for a good formula).

- **exercise regularly:** moving the body gets a good flow of blood through the liver and activates its functioning. You don't have to do a lot but it will make an enormous difference to how your body functions.

How do you get your liver to function well? Follow the guidelines on page 30. Also, avoid drinking alcohol so long as your energies are depleted or unstable.

Even once your energy has been restored it is a good idea to be careful about how much alcohol you consume. It is better to take alcohol in small quantities only and periodically rather than every day. If you really value a high-energy way of life you might consider replacing alcohol altogether with other things you enjoy – like dancing for instance or laughing, or making love. When you do drink alcohol, support your liver using the special liver helpers listed on page 31. They can also be useful in improving sluggish liver function while energy levels are still low.

Under the Weather

Next time you feel out of sorts and somebody suggests it might be the weather, don't scoff. Weather changes can also steal our energy. Age-old beliefs that 'ill winds' bring sickness, odd behaviour and general misery have been supported by studies from all over the world correlating the presence of a high level of positively charged ions in the air (or an absence of negatively charged ions) with such phenomena as increased suicide rates, crimes and various illnesses including migraine, rheumatism, and nausea. This can be the result of ill winds blowing – such as the Foehn in the Alps, the Sharav in the Middle East or the Chinook in America's Rocky Mountains. Our modern concrete office buildings, furnished with synthetic materials and artificial air-conditioning, also lack negatively charged air ions. If you work in such an environment, speak to your boss about how much he can decrease absenteeism amongst his employees by installing air purifiers and ionizers.

Light Up For Energy

Light matters for energy too. When you don't get enough full-spectrum UV light entering the eyes in winter, or when you are constantly indoors, you may experience big drops in levels of melatonin – an important brain hormone which regulates our body clocks and influences our moods. This can lead to a condition known as Seasonal Affective Disorder or SAD. Your energy seems to drain away and you get depressed or suffer disturbances in sleep and appetite. The remedy? Try exposing yourself to plenty of full-spectrum light, *artificially*. Next time you replace a lighting fixture in your home or buy a desk lamp, go for one which uses full-spectrum tubes instead of the usual tungsten bulbs. If you suffer greatly from light deprivation, consider buying a full-spectrum light box. Studies have shown that exposing SAD sufferers to full-spectrum light by having them sit in front of a light box for several hours a day lifted the spirits of 60 to 80% of the people tested.

Heavy Metals and Hard Work

There are other environmental energy thieves to be wary of, such as heavy metals like lead, aluminium, and mercury from amalgam fillings. Office pollution too can be a real problem and a hard one to solve sometimes unless you succeed in making your employer aware of how employee performance can be greatly improved by providing a clean work environment. Here is a brief guide to the environmentally-based energy thieves. See which ones you think might be operating in your life and make a note in your energy workbook about how you can take action to collar them.

ENERGY DRAINERS	WHERE FOUND/SYMPTOMS	HELPFUL HINTS
Electromagnetic pollution	Caused by static from electrical appliances, VDU displays, TV, radio and portable phones, microwave ovens, electrical dial-face clocks. Symptoms include mental and emotional confusion and hormonal imbalance.	Don't sleep under an electric blanket. Unplug TV in the room in which you sleep. Sit at least 3 feet away from a VDU and 6 feet from your TV. Give away your microwave oven.
Heavy metal pollution: e.g. from lead, aluminium, mercury, cadmium	Lead from car and industrial fumes, water from lead pipes. Cooking with aluminium pots, drinking orange juice packaged in aluminium lined boxes, using certain anti-perspirants. Mercury from tinned tuna and amalgam dental fillings. Cadmium from instant/non-organic coffee and other crops grown on contaminated soils. Heavy metals interfere with energy-producing enzymes in the body leading to fatigue as well as mental and physical disorders.	Replace aluminium cooking pots/kettles. Drink spring water such as Volvic. Use sea algae supplements and add seaweed to soups and salads to chelate (bind) and eliminate the metals. Eat apples (pectin helps bind and remove heavy metals from the body).
Weather	Unusual winds and shifting barometric pressure cause depletion in negative ions resulting in depression, fatigue, irritable behaviour. Lack of adequate UV light, such as during the winter, causes Seasonal Affective Disorder (SAD).	Use an ionizer in the room in which you work and by your bed at night. Consider full-spectrum lighting.

ENERGY DRAINERS	WHERE FOUND/SYMPTOMS	HELPFUL HINTS
Office pollution	Concrete buildings, plastic furniture, and synthetic decor deplete negative ions. Stale air recycled through conditioning and heating systems contains bacteria which challenge the immune system. VDUs (see above). Fluorescent lighting disturbs the nervous system, photocopier and printer chemicals cause allergic reactions. General office pollution symptoms: fatigue, headaches, irritated eyes, skin rashes.	Use ionizers and replace fluorescent strip lights with full-spectrum ones. Keep photocopiers and printers in a room separate from the one in which you work. Take a break from your VDU for a few minutes every hour. Use radiation control screens.

Addictions and Life Squanderers

It is not only environmental influences which drain energy – so can the way we live our lives. Most of us, whether or not we are aware of it, carry around our own brand of addictions, whether they be to chocolate chip cookies, television, work or sex. Addictions are what I call 'lifestyle energy drainers'. They squander energy like little else. Ask any doctor about addiction. He will tell you it involves a substance or a form of behaviour which is used compulsively, which alters behaviour and which causes unpleasant symptoms when access to it is denied. Alcohol, substance abuse, addictive eating behaviour, drugs and work-compulsion have been shown to lie beneath a wide range of chronic health problems and social ills. 60% of long-term patients in mental institutions in the West are there because of drug and alcohol problems and almost 40% of our hospital admissions are directly related to addiction. Addiction of one kind or another is our third greatest killer, coming after only cancer and heart disease.

Becoming aware of any addictions in your own life, whatever they may be, is the first step to reclaiming energy wasted on them. It may surprise you but an addiction is really a storeroom for your own power and energy that is just waiting to be accessed. Overcoming an addiction, whether it is major or minor, can be an exciting challenge on the way to claiming more of your personal power and releasing life energy. Of course it isn't easy. Denying yourself something which your body has come to depend on is never fun. But with the right approach you can transform the symptoms of withdrawal into steps that lead you towards richness and a sense of satisfaction in your life.

At the centre of most addictive behaviour lies a feeling of guilt and powerlessness. Both of these are massive energy drainers. Identifying your own addictions is a vital part of tapping into more potential life energy. When you are addicted to something your ability to experience the full range of sensory delight in what you do, see, touch, smell and taste is undermined. After all, you can only fully appreciate the smouldering bitterness of the finest chocolate when you are *not* a chocoholic.

Possible Addictive Substances
sugar, chocolate, ice cream, biscuits (and any other sweets or any other food), coffee, alcohol, cigarettes, mild narcotics such as marijuana, tranquillizers . . .

Possible Forms of Addictive Behaviour
working, shopping, sex, falling in love, watching television, eating . . .

Addiction Scanning

Get out your energy workbook. Now look at the definition of addiction below and apply to it any substances or behaviours you think you might be addicted to – even in a mild way – and then record what you find:

> The dependence on a substance or form of behaviour which is used compulsively and produces a feeling of satisfaction and/or a psychic drive. When access is denied to the addictive element, cravings and unpleasant physical and/or psychological symptoms of withdrawal occur.

Once you have identified any suspect addiction use the questions below to determine the severity of your addiction and help you become aware of just how much of your energy – both mental and physical – goes into feeding the addiction.

The questions are formulated around the term 'crutch' to stand for either an addictive substance or an addictive form of behaviour.

Answer each of the following questions (A), (B) or (C):
(A) = Almost always (B) = Sometimes (C) = Never

☐ Do you suffer from low self-esteem and feel unable to cope with many of the pressures of your life?

☐ When you find yourself challenged by a stressful situation do you automatically turn to your crutch?

☐ Do you find yourself thinking about when you will next be able to have your crutch throughout the day?

☐ Do you get nervous or anxious at the thought of being deprived of your crutch?

☐ When you use the crutch do you feel better and does it bring you a sense of comfort almost immediately?

☐ Do you find it difficult to stop taking it/doing it once you start?

☐ Do you find yourself feeling guilty about it?

☐ Are you defensive when anyone seems to criticize your use of it?

☐ When you feel down or lonely or depressed or anxious or upset do you automatically reach for the crutch?

☐ Do you suffer withdrawal symptoms such as depression, irritability or headaches when you don't have the crutch for a few hours/a few days?

If you answered mostly (C) to the above questions then addiction probably inhibits your life energy very little. Lucky you!

If you answered mostly (B) then your addiction is moderate and your energy levels could be increased to some extent by cutting down on or eliminating your crutch.

If you answered mostly (A) then your addiction is significant and your energy considerably drained by it. You could benefit greatly from overcoming it and eliminating the crutch (or the compulsive use of it) from your life.

If you do identify addictions in your life the next move is to get help. If your addiction is food-related you could well have a food allergy – for foods or drinks, including alcohol, to which you are addicted often have an allergic component. (Read more about identifying these addictions and handling them in the next chapter.) If your addictions are behavioural there are two things which can be enormously helpful in sorting them out. Firstly, take steps to 'follow your bliss' more and more in your life and learn to listen better to the whispers of your soul. Secondly, get in touch with one of the really useful organizations, many of which have been fashioned after Alcoholics Anonymous and whose aim is to help people rechannel their life energies and clear their addictions (see Resources, p. 148). Here are a few more of the lifestyle energy drainers. How many of them operate in your life?

Lifestyle Energy Drainers		
Convenience Foods	Processed foods contain altered fats, refined flour and sugar, as well as artificial additives, flavourings and preservatives, all of which provoke biochemical chaos and can result in mental confusion and depression, bad skin and increased susceptibility to illness as well as degenerative conditions.	Buy foods that are as close as possible to their natural state. Eat a good portion of your food raw. Go organic.
Addictions	Addictions to substances such as cigarettes, narcotics, alcohol, chocolate, sugar or caffeine upset the body's metabolic balance, depleting it of essential nutrients and leading to chronic fatigue. They also waste energy by channelling it into dead ends instead of freeing it and enabling you to make creative use of it.	Acknowledge your cravings as an addiction.
Overeating	Eating more than your body needs stresses the digestive system, depleting enzymes so that foods are badly broken down and poorly absorbed – deficiencies result. Digestion in itself requires tremendous amounts of energy and eating too often and too much causes fatigue.	Eliminate cravings and false hunger by getting rid of junk foods and combining your foods well. Look out for food allergies and get rid of them. Ask yourself what dissatisfaction in your life overeating is masking, and take steps to find a solution.

Crash Dieting	Fad diets are poorly balanced and deplete the body of vital nutrients, often resulting in fatigue and deficiency diseases such as anaemia. They also make you fat and flabby as you regain the weight you lost.	Look to a high-raw, well-combined way of eating and find a form of exercise that inspires you if you want to shed excess weight permanently. Honour your body, not some phantom image from a glossy magazine, and start to listen to what *it* wants.
Sedentary Lifestyle	Undermines your body's potential to produce electromagnetic energy and can result in calcium and magnesium being leached from your bones and tissues. This can wreak havoc with nails and hair, too. It can also deplete you of hormones needed to prevent premature ageing and can encourage depression.	Get physical by walking briskly in comfortable shoes for 1/2 an hour a day, or dance, or swim, or run regularly and see how quickly you feel the difference.

The Sneaky Inner Thieves

Negative emotions like fear, resentment, depression and low self-esteem wipe out our life energy – especially when they are long-term and especially when they remain unconscious. So does compromising yourself by living your life by somebody else's rules rather than your own. There is nothing particularly energy-draining about a good bout of anger if it is felt consciously and expressed but when anger turns inward it can become resentment which gets filed away deep within us – sometimes so far down we are not even conscious that it is there. Then our basic life force and creativity become hampered and energy-depleting psychological states come into play. We can experience long-term hopelessness or depression, bouts of anxiety and also physical illness. Unhappiness and lack of passion for life undermines energy badly. It is important to become aware of whether these things are operating in your life and if so how. Back to your energy workbook. Read on and see if any of the following applies to you. Make notes about your emotional energy thieves so you can begin transforming them into creative power.

Anxiety Waste

Few emotions drain vitality like anxiety. While you dash about (either physically or in your mind) feeling unsafe and unstable and trying like mad to make everything seem all right, you waste enormous amounts of energy. Living with anxiety often leads to nothing ever being fully achieved. This in turn results in further anxiety and further depletion of energy.

Wherever there is anxiety there is a high level of electrical, electro-positive magnetic activity and chemical acidity in the body. This affects the sympathetic nervous system and encourages further feelings of fear, irritability, nausea, headache, as well as an inability to concentrate, and can produce muscle pain and insomnia. Even minor attacks of nervousness can dramatically undermine your work performance and make it almost impossible to enjoy yourself. Chronic anxiety in someone's life is frequently related to food allergies. Re-aligning your diet can help a lot with it. So can physical exercise which calms electrical and chemical over-activity, replacing them with more balanced energy.

Get into Anger

Resentment is another big energy blocker. Anger immediately felt and expressed keeps energy flowing. Think of when you were a child and you got angry at a friend. It was quick to come and quick to pass so you could get on

41

with whatever you both were doing. As adults we tend to swallow our anger, turning it into resentment. Anger in itself does not drain energy, it can be the driving force to achieving a goal. But when anger is held in, it can turn into depression or resentment – both huge energy thieves.

Harboured resentment corrupts your view of life and of yourself. Getting rid of this energy drainer means taking a long hard look at the resentments in your life and gradually letting go of them.

Get out your workbook and write a letter to any person towards whom you feel particularly resentful or angry (or even write to 'life itself'). List all of their offences and tell them exactly how you feel about them. Then, when you are ready (it may be now or it may be six weeks from now), at the bottom of the letter write: 'I, (your name), hereby forgive you (the person's name) entirely for the above grievances. In so doing I bless you and wish you well and release all my ill feelings.' When you have finished, read this letter out loud to yourself. Then leave it behind – or tear it out and burn it.

What Do You Fear?

Fear also blocks energy. In a measurable physical way it freezes you into inactivity and makes all things seem impossible. Chronic fear, usually unconscious, can lead you to make the wrong choices because you feel the need continually to compromise on fundamental issues such as what you really want and value. This is dangerous thinking in energy terms. When you feel low in energy you tend to attract energy drainers which in turn attract other energy drainers and before you know it you find yourself caught up and helpless – a victim to circumstances over which you have no power. Becoming aware of your fears and just writing them down in your workbook can help diffuse a lot of their power. If they are very great, get professional help for them from a counsellor.

How About Depression?

Depression is believed to be the most common cause of chronic fatigue. Like anxiety it can sometimes grow out of a biochemical imbalance. For example, living on a diet of processed convenience foods depletes your body of the minerals essential for its energy-transmitting pathways and for brain-chemicals like noradrenaline that are needed to keep your spirits high. Sometimes depression develops as a result of blocked emotions which you may not even be aware you are feeling – like grief or sadness. Often depression arises when you turn your anger in on yourself in a misguided attempt to stop yourself from doing harm to anyone. In any case, once you feel depression, you get caught up in a vicious circle where your low-energy state only further feeds the negative state and vice versa. Women are particularly prone to this energy thief.

Always where long-term depression is present a person's creative power is blocked. This is something that I know a lot about since in my early twenties I suffered from depression badly. It was the kind of depression which appeared to have no specific cause – the kind for which the doctor suggests either anti-depressant drugs or psychotherapy. Anti-depressant drugs are not only

---

Women and Depression

According to recent research, women are twice as susceptible to depression as men. One obvious factor is the female biological make-up with its hormonal cycles that contribute to mood swings. But there are also social factors. According to the American Psychological Association, the structure of our society, which tends to place women in more passive roles than men, creates a sense of impotence, making women more prone to dissatisfaction and depression. The APA's Task Force on Women and Depression also found that 37% of the women suffering from depression that were studied had been victims of significant physical or sexual abuse by the age of 21.

---

dangerous because of their side effects: they also, I believe, miss the point. You do not want to cover over depression, you want to release the energy locked within yourself so it can be transmuted into creativity in your life.

To achieve this try a fresh approach:

1. Unlock your imagination so that you begin to see depression not as an illness or insurmountable obstacle in your life but rather as something for you to work with and transform so that the energy trapped beneath it can be freed for creative use.

2. Alter the way you are living by detoxifying your body (see Step 5), identifying and clearing away any biochemical problems such as food allergies or candida overgrowths (see Step 4), and then slowly, yet with determination, building a new lifestyle for yourself that serves your purposes – whatever they may be.

3. Find a creative outlet for the energies that emerge and be willing to listen to what they are telling you even if it means changing things in your life such as a job or relationship that is not working.

Here is a list of some specific emotional energy thieves. How many apply to you? Record your responses in your workbook.

Emotional Energy Snatchers		
Draining relationships	Any relationship based on illusions that each person has about the other wastes a great deal of energy. Such relationships often involve a sense of being crushed or held back by the other person.	As you clear away old perceptions and ideas you are more able to recognize any relationship that doesn't serve you, and adjust it to fit the real you or else spend less time with the person concerned.

Fear	Freezes you into inactivity and avoidance. Forces you to make compromising life choices. Inhibits the immune system, making you more susceptible to illness.	Identify your fears by writing them down. Decide which are valid and take action to allay them.
Compromise	Continually sacrificing your own needs or desires in favour of what others want from you, or what you believe is required of you socially, drains energy.	Identify the signs of compromise such as your use of the words 'I should' and 'I feel guilty if I don't'. Pause before you promise to do something you don't want to do and think again.
Resentment	Feeling wronged by someone can lock you into a self-limiting, energy-blocking prison.	Express your feelings of anger or pain directly to the person concerned. If this isn't practical or appropriate, try writing them a letter (see page 42).
Depression	Suppresses metabolic processes, decreases energy levels, lowers self-esteem.	Check out your diet for sensitivities, start exercising and try out some of the herbal helpers (see page 149)
Low self-esteem	Lack of self-esteem encourages a defeatist/victim attitude which drains energy. It also invites a lack of respect and appreciation from others around you.	Take a good look at the reasons you devalue yourself and ask if they are valid. Then write a list of your achievements and good qualities. Make a conscious effort to acknowledge these. Take action to increase your self-esteem – take up exercise.

From a physical point of view there are some wonderful natural substances and plant helpers you can make friends with. You can explore what they have to offer you in helping to shift emotional gears should you find yourself plagued by depression, anxiety, fear or low self-esteem. Here are some of my favourites:

- **GABA** *Gamma-aminobuteric acid* is a natural metabolite – a substance found in the body – which your body makes from the amino acid l-glutamine. It is important for brain chemistry since it has a calming ability. So important are its actions that many of the most well-known drugs used to treat both anxiety and insomnia work by triggering the receptor sites for GABA in the brain, thereby calming the nervous system. Some nutritionally orientated physicians swear by its ability to help in cases of depression and anxiety. It is usually given in doses of 250mg of GABA on an empty stomach (to increase its ability to cross the blood-brain barrier) four times a day.

- **St John's Wort** *Hypericum perforatum* is the centuries-old wise-woman herbal remedy for female depression. Researchers who evaluated depressed women given 300mg of the St John's Wort extract discovered that many of the negative feelings that accompany depression – from lack of self-worth or moodiness to continual sleepiness and anxiety – were significantly alleviated by taking the herb. According to an interesting German study, when a standardized extract of the plant was given to women there was a significant increase in the levels of *dopamine* excreted in their urine. St John's Wort apparently increases the production of this important brain chemical, higher levels of which are associated with freedom from depression and lower levels with depression itself. Many of the most powerful anti-depressant drugs, such as imprimine and amitriptyline, aim to increase the levels of dopamine in the body. The only difference is that whereas prescription drugs carry the risk of serious side effects, St John's Wort does not.

- **Siberian Ginseng** *Eleutherococcus senticosus* is not a real ginseng at all but rather an adaptogenic plant which has been well tested by Russian scientists for its ability to enhance people's stamina, increase resistance to illness and heighten energy over a long period of time. It is also useful for chronic depression, anxiety, fear and low self-esteem. When people take it they feel better – probably because it improves the balance between various important neurotransmitters in the brain, including dopamine and noradrenaline, and thereby improves mood. (See Resources, p. 149.)

- **Kava** *Piper methysticum* is a root used in the South Pacific to make a popular drink which for centuries people have taken in order to calm themselves and to promote good will and peace between friends and neighbours. It is a wonderful plant: it really does impart a sense of peaceful contentment and is especially good for counteracting the negative blocked feeling that comes with depression and anxiety. The plant has been much studied in an attempt to identify its active compounds and understand its pharmacological effects. The most significant of its ingredients appears to be *kava alpha-pyrones* although other plant chemicals also contribute to its calming actions. In animal experiments these compounds have been shown to act as sedatives, pain relievers and muscle-relaxants. They appear to exert their psychological benefits by affecting the limbic system – that primitive part of the brain considered to be the centre of emotions. Kava is also now believed to have an ability to protect the brain against damage from low levels of oxygen. In humans it has been used successfully to treat depression, nervousness, insomnia and to improve memory. In one study a purified form of its most active ingredient was compared to a common tranquillizer drug over a period of several weeks. Researchers reported that Kava was equally effective in eliminating anxiety, yet while the drug was associated with addictive side effects, the Kava extract showed none (see Resources, p. 150).

Now let's ferret out the biochemical energy thieves and set them running.

Step Four
Face the Body Snatchers

In Charles Dickens' *A Christmas Carol*, Jacob Marley, Scrooge's dead partner, appears to him as a ghost:

> 'You don't believe in me,' observed the Ghost. 'I don't,' said Scrooge. 'What evidence would you have of my reality beyond that of your senses?' 'I don't know,' said Scrooge. 'Why do you doubt your senses?' 'Because', said Scrooge, 'a little thing affects them. A slight disorder of the stomach makes them cheat. You may be an undigested bit of beef, a blot of mustard, a crumb of cheese, a fragment of an underdone potato. There's more of gravy than of grave about you, whatever you are!'

Scrooge was right. Biochemical changes brought about by what you eat, how well you eat, and how often you eat, can affect your brain and alter consciousness, producing imaginary fears – even, for some people, hallucinations – and can cause depression and anxiety as well as chronic fatigue. Let's look at some of the energy-sensitive nutrition-related areas which affect mind, body and spirit and at what can be done to overcome them. Ask yourself how many of them apply to your life and let's see what can be done to eliminate them.

Check out Your Blood Sugar

A common energy drainer is low blood sugar – known as *reactive hypoglycaemia*. It happens when your body is not able to metabolize carbohydrate efficiently and is often the result of years lived on convenience foods, most of which are stuffed with hidden sugars and refined flour.

Carbohydrates are essential to provide us with the energy we need. But for high-level, lasting energy you need to choose the right kind. Complex carbohydrates such as whole-grains, brown rice, vegetables, fruits, and whole-grain breads are the real energy-makers. They come as nature packaged them complete with natural fibre, essential fatty acids, and important vitamins and minerals which the body needs to make use of them. Complex carbohydrates are absorbed *slowly*, providing a steady stream of energy in the form of glucose throughout the day so you can carry on doing whatever you are doing without fatigue. These are 'good guy' carbs.

Refined or simple carbohydrates like white bread, white rice, most breakfast cereals and sugars are the bad guys. Because they have been stripped of their natural fibre as well as many – sometimes all – of the minerals, trace elements and vitamins you need, they are absorbed very quickly into your bloodstream, upsetting the pancreas and disrupting the steady flow of life energy in your body.

Simple Disasters

In the West we consume an astounding one-third of our calories in the form of refined sugar. Many experts believe that, as a result, between 65 and 80% of us experience blood sugar problems.

Like cocaine – the deadly white powder refined from the innocuous coca plant – refined sugar consumed in such quantities can result in a kind of addiction, where you experience energy surges and slumps throughout the day which have you reaching for a chocolate bar or cup of strong coffee to keep you going. Each time we eat sugar it does two things. Firstly, it depletes our bodies of essential nutrients such as chromium which are needed for its metabolism. As a result deficiencies in these elements gradually develop in us and certain metabolic processes become impaired so that the body's energy-producing capacities become grossly diminished. Secondly, it has a negative effect on the body's blood sugar regulation systems.

Glucose is the body's primary source of energy, and is especially important for brain function. We need to maintain our levels of glucose in the blood within a very narrow range. But drinking drinks or eating foods which contain glucose is, strangely enough, the worst thing you can do to accomplish this. To balance blood sugar the body uses a number of elaborate feedback mechanisms and is highly dependent upon the secretion of appropriate quantities of insulin. When sugar levels get too high a release of insulin from the pancreas brings them back down within the normal range.

Pancreatic Burnout

This is all well and good when you are eating slow-release complex carbohydrates. But when you eat refined sugar over and over again this can produce a trigger-happy pancreas which keeps pouring out insulin to try to regulate glucose levels in the blood, and produces blood sugar chaos. In time this way of eating can actually exhaust the pancreas altogether. The result? Chronic fatigue, through chronic reactive hypoglycaemia, plus all sorts of symptoms that can come with it. In some people, low blood sugar can bring about the onset of diabetes.

Here are a few of the common symptoms associated with low blood sugar:

● blurred vision
● depression
● headaches
● anxiety and irritability
● excessive sweating
● bizarre behaviour
● mental confusion
● aches and pains in joints
● chronic fatigue
● speech disturbances

When hypoglycaemia was first brought to the attention of the general public back in the 1970s those doctors who had little knowledge of how nutrition affects health pooh-poohed the idea that it could exist, let alone be responsible for so many symptoms. Now even the average doctor has become aware that refined carbohydrates are not good for human health, that there is a strong correlation between their consumption and disturbed blood sugar regulation, and – most important of all – that simple changes in diet can for most people remedy the situation quite easily over a period of a few weeks or months.

How Low Can You Go?

How do you check out whether or not you are experiencing low blood sugar? There is a medical test your doctor can carry out called a 6-hour glucose tolerance test. After fasting you for 12 hours, your doctor measures your blood sugar level by taking blood from your arm. Then he or she will give you a glucose drink. After this, every hour for six hours – and it *has* to be this long to get an accurate assessment of the situation, although some doctors are still not aware of this – more blood is taken from you and blood sugar is checked again. If blood sugar levels fall below 50ml per decilitre this indicates hypoglycaemia. So does a decrease of 20 milligrams or more from the measurement at fasting, together with certain unusual changes in blood sugar.

The trouble is that not only is such a test lengthy and costly, but experts in blood sugar analysis now insist that blood sugar problems can be present in people even when their glucose levels are above 50mg per decilitre. This is because a good number of the symptoms associated with hypoglycaemia can also be triggered by an overactive pancreas that secretes too much insulin, or even by an excess of adrenaline from prolonged stress. As a result nutritionally orientated doctors now also check for insulin and adrenaline levels, all of which becomes even more time-consuming and costly.

Try the Self-Check Blood Sugar Quiz

Many nutritionally trained doctors who work with the diagnosis and treatment of hypoglycaemia prefer to use a simple questionnaire that looks at symptoms. It goes something like this.

Get out your energy workbook and take the simple test below to see if hypoglycaemia might be affecting your energy levels.

Mark each box with a score of 1–3: 1 = sometimes: 2 = often: 3 = frequently.

☐ 1. Do you crave sweets?

☐ 2. Are you irritable if you skip a meal?

☐ 3. Do you feel tired if you skip a meal?

☐ 4. Do you feel tired an hour or so after a meal?

☐ 5. Are you dizzy if you suddenly stand up?

☐ 6. Do you have an energy slump in the afternoon?

☐ 7. Do you get frequent headaches?

☐ 8. Do you experience heart palpitations?

☐ 9. Do you have blurred vision?

☐ 10. Is your memory poor?

☐ 11. Are you anxious or nervous?

☐ 12. Do you have mood swings?

Add up your score and make a note of it in your workbook. You may want to take the test again in a month or so. If it is less than 5 you are unlikely to have to worry about your blood sugar. If it is between 5 and 14 blood sugar irregularities are likely. If it is above 14 you will need to take action to regulate your blood sugar levels.

The good news about low blood sugar is that if you suspect you have it, the dietary changes needed to clear it are bound to do you good whether you have low blood sugar or not. Here they are:

Banish coffee, cut out refined foods including sugars and fruit juices, and eat only small quantities of fruit. Get into a high-energy way of eating such as that outlined in Bite into Energy (Step 6). Within a few weeks those energy lumps and bumps will disappear as your body re-establishes good metabolic balance. One more thing: consider supplementing your diet from a good chromium source every day.

Chromium is a gift from the gods when it comes to overcoming hypoglycaemia. Nutrition experts recommend taking supplements of either chromium polynicotinate or chromium picolinate. Chromium is the trace element which lies at the core of what is known as the glucose tolerance factor in the body. Gradually depleted over years of eating convenience foods high in refined carbohydrates and sugar, chromium supplies can be rebuilt gradually through supplemention. 200mcg is usually recommended taken one to three times a day.

Thyroid Threats

Another body-based energy snatcher is *hypothyroidism*. As well as chronic fatigue, some of our most common problems – chronic headaches, falling hair, skin troubles, and even a tendency towards infections – can be the result of low thyroid functioning.

The thyroid, which weighs less than 30g, is the small butterfly-shaped gland in the neck that, under the direction of the pituitary and hypothalamus, is responsible for regulating energy production and consumption in the body. The minute quantity of hormones which this gland produces (less than a spoonful a year) stimulate an enormous number of activities in your body – from increasing the oxygen consumption of every cell to encouraging protein synthesis needed to repair damaged tissue. The trouble is that the standard blood tests most doctors use often miss mild hypothyroidism, which can be a major concern when going for a high-energy lifestyle. For if your thyroid is chronically under-active this can render useless almost anything you do to help increase your energy levels. Hypothyroidism has been described as trying to run your car without a fuel pump – there may be plenty of petrol but it is not getting to the engine.

Check out Your Thyroid

The thyroid gland regulates metabolism in every cell of your body and has a lot to say about how much energy you have in your life. When your thyroid gland is under-active this can predispose your body to a lot of undesirable effects:

- overweight caused by slow fat burning
- dry skin
- dry, coarse hair and hair loss
- constipation
- thin or brittle nails often with transverse grooves
- depression, together with weakness and fatigue
- shortness of breath
- high cholesterol and triglyceride levels
- capillary damage, water retention and cellulite
- loss of sex drive
- infertility, premature birth and stillbirths

Low thyroid function is an important condition to recognize and eliminate if you are chronically tired. Yet it often goes unrecognized by doctors probably because, unless they are trained in natural medicine, they tend to rely on blood measurements of thyroid hormone levels for its diagnosis. According to experts in thyroid disorders, blood tests often miss identifying the condition – especially when it is in a milder form.

Hypothyroidism, like depression, is particularly common in women, and it is important not to overlook it. For when it is present, basic actions you may take to bring high levels of energy into your life will be undermined. It would be rather like trying to make a car run properly if the carburettor was not working. Since thyroid hormones control the body's metabolic rate, and since body temperature is an important indicator of your rate of metabolism, nutritionally aware doctors use a simple, yet highly revealing do-it-yourself method of temperature taking to identify when the thyroid is under-active. Here's how:

Do-It-Yourself Thyroid Check

- Before you slip into bed shake down a thermometer to below 92°F and place it beside your bed.
- In the morning as soon as you awaken slip the thermometer under your arm and let it rest in your naked armpit for a full ten minutes.
- Stay as quiet as you can during this time, with your eyes closed, just resting.
- Read your temperature and record it along with the date in your workbook.
- Repeat the same procedure for at least 3 – preferably 5 – mornings in a row, ideally at the same time each day. (Do not carry out this procedure during the first three days of your menstrual period, but any other time will do.)
- Normal basal body temperature is between 97.6°F and 98.2°F. If your temperatures are lower than that this may reflect hypothyroidism and require that you see a doctor – preferably one who is aware of the work of doctors such as Broda Barnes (see Further Reading, p. 155).
- The best treatment consists of using a supplement either of specific thyroid hormones or (far better) whole thyroid (such as Armour Thyroid) daily, although in some people dietary improvement itself, plus regular exercise, can enormously improve hypothyroidism.

Are You Yeast Free?

Yeast is another energy-sapper. The common yeast Candida albicans lives harmlessly in the gastrointestinal tract of all of us, along with a lot of other micro-organisms, some of which actually support high-level health. Candida is the yeast which, if it proliferates in the vaginal tract, can cause thrush. Under certain circumstances candida overgrowth occurs to produce a complex medical syndrome known as the *yeast syndrome* or *chronic candidiasis*. Common symptoms frequently traced back to overgrowth of candida in the gut include loss of energy, chronic fatigue, decreased libido, bloating and wind, depression and irritability, inability to concentrate, low immune function which makes you susceptible to colds

---

Candida Overgrowth Factors

Here are some factors which are most common in people with chronic yeast syndrome. Do many of these apply to you?

- Impaired immune function
- Sensitivity to dampness and smells
- Emotional mood swings, confusion and depression
- Recurrent vaginal yeast in women and recurrent problems in the prostate in men
- Long-term use of the Pill in women
- Frequent use of cortisone-related drugs and ulcer drugs
- Frequent or long-term use of antibiotics for recurrent infections or the treatment of acne
- Chronic digestive problems such as bloating or wind
- Food reactions such as food allergies
- Long-term fatigue
- Recurrent skin fungus problems such as athlete's foot, or nail problems or genital itching
- Cravings for sweets, breads or alcohol
- Insufficient digestive secretions
- Eating a lot of sugar
- Diabetes mellitus
- Lack of digestive enzymes

---

and 'flu, food sensitivities and cravings for foods rich in carbohydrates or yeast.

Some of the situations which encourage the proliferation of candida include the taking of broad-spectrum antibiotics and other drugs, the presence of diabetes, eating a lot of sugar, not having sufficient digestive secretions, and taking the Pill. All of these things create an internal environment in your body which encourages this yeast/fungus to burgeon.

A medical diagnosis of chronic candidiasis is difficult to make because there is no single specific diagnostic test for it and because many doctors still know very little about it. However, there are also some common symptoms that give a strong indication of whether or not there is a candida overgrowth in your body. Take out your workbook and go through the little test below.

Check Your Symptoms

Score yourself: 1 = seldom; 2 = sometimes; 3 = often. Ignore those which do not apply to you. Record your points total in your energy workbook then go on to the next quiz.

☐ low libido	☐ light-headedness
☐ PMS	☐ mood swings
☐ tummy pain	☐ poor concentration
☐ muscle or joint aches	☐ heartburn
☐ flagging memory	☐ dry mouth
☐ exhaustion	☐ cough
☐ depression	☐ recurrent infections
☐ drowsiness	☐ impotence
☐ headaches	☐ muscle weakness
☐ indigestion	☐ tingling or numbness

☐ diarrhoea ☐ blurred vision

☐ genital itch ☐ menstrual irregularities

Past Imperfect

Now let's look at your present and your past. For each yes answer to the questions below, add ten points.

☐ Are you a sugar lover?

☐ Do you reach for one biscuit and find yourself eating the whole pack?

☐ Do you react badly to the smell of perfumes?

☐ Do you take or have you taken the Pill?

☐ Have you taken or are you taking HRT?

☐ Have you ever taken broad-spectrum antibiotics for more than 10 days?

☐ Do you crave alcohol?

☐ Do you feel worse when the weather is damp or you are in a damp house?

☐ Does cigarette smoke make you feel unwell?

☐ Have you ever had athlete's foot or fungal infections on hands or skin?

Now total the number of points from both quizzes and record it in your workbook.

If your score is less than 60, candida overgrowth is unlikely to be a problem for you. Between 60 and 100, you probably have more candida in your body than is healthy, but staying away from sugar, sweets and too much fruit may well be enough to clear it within a few weeks. If your score is above 100 you may need to take serious action to clear candida from your system.

The good news is that most of the things you can do to improve the overall quality of your diet, such as cutting out junk fats, sugar and highly processed foods (all of which candida thrives on), alter the internal environment and discourage the proliferation of this yeast/fungus. However, if you suspect a significant level of candidiasis, experts offer advice which is useful to follow since it does not contradict the general guidelines for good eating and has made an enormous difference in the lives of many people who have been made miserable by this condition:

- **Drop the drugs:** Don't take antibiotics, steroids, birth control pills, or standard drug-based HRT (unless there is a real medical necessity).
- **Change your diet:** Don't feed candida on foods it thrives on. This means avoid like the plague any refined carbohydrate foods like white flour, refined sugars such as corn syrup and glucose, fruit juices and honey. Also steer clear of milk products, baked foods made with wheat flour, and all foods to which you suspect you might be allergic or sensitive.
- **Never eat foods which may have a high yeast content:** Avoid alcohol, cheese, peanuts, dried fruits, grapes and yeast breads.
- **Eat lots of fresh vegetables** (except yams, parsnips, corn and potatoes): Eat as much as you like of fish and game, lamb and whole grains except wheat.
- **Limit fruits:** to no more than two pieces a day chosen from apples, berries, pears and bananas until symptoms have gone.
- **Check for food sensitivities:** Food sensitivities are common with candida. The things you crave are frequently what the yeast itself craves. Try to identify any possible sensitivities and weed them out. This can help a lot.
- **Drink Pau d'Arco:** This tea from the South American tree has a long folk use in the treatment of infections probably thanks to its *lapachol* content. Both lapachol and other compounds from Pau d'Arco have demonstrated anti-candida effects. Drink some several times a day. See Resources, page 150.

- **Add a grapefruit seed extract:** and a good probiotic supplement to your diet.
- **Go for help:** If these things do not make a significant difference then seek out a good nutritionist or nutritionally orientated doctor who is genuinely knowledgeable about the treatment of candida. It is not enough simply to give a fungicidal drug which is the usual treatment. While it can suppress the candida when you are taking it, often when you stop doing so it regrows so you are soon back to where you started.
- **Take heart:** Once the candida is under control you will probably be able to eat everything you like so long as you continue to steer clear of unnecessary drugs and highly processed convenience foods. But be patient. It takes time for nature to balance your body from inside out.

Anti-Candida Foods – Stress These in Your Diet

meats (preferably organic)	pulses
chicken	nuts and seeds
turkey	butter
eggs	extra virgin olive oil
fish	lemon
whole grains except wheat	2 pieces of fruit

Foods to avoid while you are clearing possible candida infestation

sugar in any form
fruit juices
dried fruits
honey
baked goods containing yeast or made from wheat flour
simple carbohydrates such as most breakfast cereals, white
    bread, white rice and pasta
mushrooms
cheeses
vinegars
alcoholic drinks

Food Sensitivities

Sometimes called food intolerance or even food allergies, these sensitivities, which were first identified way back in the 1930s by the famous allergist Dr Albert Rowe, are an alarmingly common cause of chronic fatigue. Rowe called the kind of chronic fatigue which arises from food allergies – and often includes muscle and joint aches, depression, sleepiness and poor concentration – *allergic toremia*. Later he realized how widespread this condition is and renamed it *allergic tension-fatigue syndrome*. Today, unfortunately, many doctors faced with chronic fatigue in their patients forget that somewhere between 50 and 85% of these people, when tested, will be found to be food-allergic.

Allergy with a Difference

Food allergies are quite different from ordinary allergies, where you have an antibody response to something you have come into contact with. The curious thing about food sensitivity is that often what you happen to be allergic to, whether it be wheat or alcohol or chocolate, you will find you have a *craving* for. It works like this. When you are sensitive to a food or chemical, on first contact you will react negatively to it. But if you use it or are exposed to it continually these symptoms become masked. Then, like the alcoholic who feels OK so long as he has a drink in his hand, so long as you continue to be exposed to it you can avoid the first negative reaction. But then when it is eliminated from your diet, WHAM – you get withdrawal symptoms. Frequently, this kind of allergy-cum-addiction is the hidden cause behind the 'eat one biscuit, eat the packet' syndrome. Wheat is one of the most common foods to which people are allergic.

Food allergies happen when for any number of reasons your body reacts badly to the food you eat. This reaction may or may not be mediated by the immune system and therefore may or may not be picked up by a doctor trained in traditional methods of spotting allergies.

Beware Leaky Gut

Many things can cause a bad reaction to food. It can be a response to the protein or starch or additives the food contains (such as colourings or preservatives). In some cases it is a high sensitivity or a drug-like reaction to the food. In others the intestinal mucosa may become damaged causing what is known as *leaky gut syndrome*, where long chain proteins or starches or unwanted chemicals are drawn straight through the gut wall into the bloodstream where they have no business to be.

Food allergies used to be relatively uncommon. Now they are becoming so widespread that many nutritionally trained doctors estimate that more than 50% of people in the Western world suffer from symptoms associated with food reactions. There are probably two reasons for this. Firstly, our immune systems are increasingly challenged by the presence of chemical and energetic pollution in our environment, while the massive consumption of convenience foods has rendered large segments of the population deficient in minerals and vitamins which help protect us from sensitivity reactions. Secondly, these same convenience foods tend to be chock-full of the food items highest on the food-sensitivity list: milk products and wheat products including flour and everything made from it. It may well be that the body's enzymes whose job it is to digest milk and wheat are therefore gravely over-taxed, and the system simply becomes overwhelmed by the amount of these two foods (that are added to just about everything because they are cheap to produce).

Tests for Food Allergies

There are various ways to find out if you are food-allergic. You can use an elimination diet which usually consists of lamb, chicken, potatoes, rice, bananas, broccoli and pears eaten with *nothing* else for a period of one or two weeks. If you are food-allergic, your symptoms should disappear by about the sixth day of the diet. After a week or two on the elimination diet you then 'challenge' your system very carefully by continuing with the same elimination diet but adding every other day a new food – on its own – to which you *suspect* you may be allergic. Then watch to see if any symptoms reappear. This takes a lot of time and care, and means recording everything in your energy workbook. Gradually, provided only one suspected food is introduced at a time, you can eventually identify the culprit foods and then eliminate them completely from your diet from then on.

Energy Soars

When you eliminate foods to which you are allergic your energy levels rise and rise. If then you suddenly introduce a food to which you are allergic you will get a reaction either immediately or within the next two to three days. Some doctors working with food allergies prefer to fast their patients for several days on pure water, and then test each food by placing a solution of it in water under the tongue of the patient and monitoring heart rate and changes in blood pressure and the appearance of either mental or physical symptoms. This method is never, I should emphasize, used for people who may have severe allergic reactions that can be life-threatening, such as asthmatic attacks.

There are also lab tests designed to identify food allergies, but they tend to be expensive and the average doctor usually knows little about them. Typical skin scratch tests used by many doctors to identify what are known as IgE allergies – that is those which involve a particular antibody – are pretty useless when it comes to checking for food allergies as they will only pick up between 10 and 15% of them.

There are other things that can give you a clue as to whether food allergies are present in your life. Very often what you crave most is what you are food-allergic or food-sensitive to. So give some thought to what you crave and make a note of those foods in your workbook now so you can check out how eliminating one or more of these foods from your diet affects your energy levels.

What Do You Crave?

Biscuits, bread, pastry and pasta? *Suspect wheat.*

Coffee or cola? Do you drink more than 2 glasses a day? *Suspect caffeine.*

Pizza, tomato sauce, spaghetti? *Suspect tomatoes.*

Orange drinks, oranges, orange sorbet? *Suspect oranges.*

Wine? *Suspect grapes, sugar or yeast.*

Chocolate? *Suspect sugar, chocolate, or processed fats.*

Cheese, butter, yoghurt? *Suspect milk.*

Ice cream or creamy desserts? *Suspect milk, sugar or junk fats.*

Digestive Enzyme Helpers

The healthy body produces its own enzymes, each of which has a specific job to do like breaking down fats or breaking down proteins or cellulose in the foods you eat. Crash dieting, chlorine in drinking water, poor eating, stress or deficiencies of specific minerals or vitamins needed for your body to produce these enzymes can mean that your enzyme supply becomes depleted and that you are therefore unable to break your foods down properly. Digestive enzymes such as amylase, protease, lipase and bromelin are essential to break down the foods you eat into usable nutrients. Supplements of these enzymes can often be especially helpful for anyone with a food allergy as well as anyone who is experiencing difficulties with digestion or chronic fatigue. (See Resources, p. 148.)

Anaemia Needs Checking

Another common cause of long-term fatigue is anaemia. Anaemia is often the result of low levels of iron which in turn produce a deficiency in haemoglobin, the iron-containing part of red blood cells responsible for carrying oxygen to the cells all over the body and for removing waste carbon dioxide from them. If you suspect anaemia, go and see your doctor and ask him or her to do a *serum ferritin* lab test to find out about your body's iron supplies. (A routine blood analysis is simply not accurate enough.) If you find you do need extra iron, be choosy about what kind you take, since many of the iron tablets you buy over the counter or which are commonly prescribed by doctors are both poorly absorbed and can cause constipation. (See Resources, p. 150.)

Source Your Iron

There are two alternatives: 'heme' iron which comes from animal sources only – especially liver – and 'non-heme' iron which comes from plants. Heme iron is much better absorbed and does not depend on having sufficient hydrochloric acid in the stomach to use it. Non-heme iron is only one-fifth as easily absorbed. It is also easily removed from the body before absorption by the presence of fibre in the diet, calcium, preservatives etc, while heme iron remains unaffected.

Eating good organic liver several times a week is about the best way of all to build your iron reserves, provided of course that you are not a vegetarian. Liver has been shown to have all sorts of blood-building and health-building properties. Liver has also proved itself useful in improving the body's ability to burn fat, enhancing liver functions as a whole and countering fatigue. In over a hundred years of use and study nobody has yet been able to identify all of the health-building compounds found in clean, natural liver. The emphasis has to be on *clean* and *healthy* since these days there are so many animals slaughtered for meat which are *not* healthy and whose livers are filled with herbicides and pesticides. When it comes to liver, if you can possibly afford it, eat organic. If you are a vegetarian, consider taking a plant-based liquid supplement. (See Resources, p. 149.)

If you are anaemic it is also a good idea to take the other blood-building nutrients in extra quantity – vitamin B12, folic acid and vitamin C as well as a good green supplement such as Pure Synergy (see Resources, p. 149).

The metabolic body snatchers can all be big energy-drainers. The annoying thing about them is that more often than not someone with one problem, say food allergies, is likely to have low blood sugar as well. That is the bad news. The good news is that what is useful in collaring one of the body snatchers will also help you get rid of another. What is good in tackling all of them is simply detoxifying your body. Let's look at that next.

Step Five
Clear Out the Junk

When we eat convenience foods over a period of time two things happen. Firstly, we end up with subclinical nutritional deficiencies of vitamins and minerals because so many essential nutrients have been lost in the processing and storage of these foods. Secondly, wastes accumulate in the tissues. It is little wonder that excess fat deposits have become such a problem as we approach the millennium. Industrial wastes fill our rivers and seas and billions of gallons of chemicals are poured on our crops and farmlands every year. Even the fat of Arctic seals has been shown to be permeated by chemical poisons such as DDT. What the body tends to do with toxic wastes is tuck them away in fat cells so the more wastes you hold in your body the more fat cells you are likely to accumulate to store them in.

Any body burdened with a high level of wastes channels much of its available energy into trying to handle these toxins rather than into keeping cells functioning efficiently and providing you with ongoing energy. In broad terms this means that you are likely to experience flagging vitality over the years and to feel that you simply can't make the effort to change things for the better. Before you do anything else on your road to creating a high-energy lifestyle, you need to junk the junk food: microwave meals, pizza rolls, highly processed breakfast cereals, pasties, cakes, biscuits, colas and diet colas, fruit drinks, flavoured yoghurts, trifles – the list is endless. Get rid of them all.

Start Junking Junk Food

We all know, deep down, what we should eat to give us plenty of energy – so why do we eat such junk? It is not just lack of willpower. You might be surprised to learn that convenience foods – junk foods – actually encourage you to eat more of them, thanks to the disruptive effects they exert on digestion and on the person as a whole. They also promote weight gain in people who have a genetic tendency to lay down fat stores. And it's not just people – this is also true of mice, rats, dogs and chimpanzees. Replace those convenience foods with simple, delicious, wholesome fare. Here is my simple beginner's guide to help you do just that. The rewards in terms of increased energy are likely to astound you.

1. Forget the Guilt

The first barrier to overcome is attitude. Your 'willpower' is not innately 'weak'. Whenever the old 'should I?/shouldn't I?' conflict arises about whether to eat or not to eat a pre-cooked ready-in-a-minute meal, remind yourself that it is quite possible your reason for wanting it may be some sort of biochemical upset in your body, a deficiency in one or other vitamin or mineral as a result of living on convenience foods for so long, or even a disturbed digestive system. When your body is in real harmony with itself you are usually indifferent to even the most voluptuous chocolate sundae. So forget the battle of the will. Stop blaming yourself and look to strengthening your overall state of health and raising your energy levels instead.

2. Look to the Rewards

Being aware of the rewards of any lifestyle change and reminding yourself of them day by day as you go along helps make the process of change easy. Here are some of the junk-free diet bonuses:

- Greater emotional balance
- Abundant energy
- Sparkling eyes and clear, glowing skin
- Strong shiny hair
- A leaner, firmer body
- A clear mind
- A fresh, positive outlook on life
- Relief from constant hunger

3. Drink like a fish

Dehydration results in your feeling weak and tired and can lead to overeating, as it disturbs your appetite mechanisms so you think you are hungry even when you are not. Drinking lots of pure, clean water detoxifies your body steadily and can help you break the junk food habit. Thoughts and feelings become distorted when your body gets even mildly dehydrated. Research with athletes at Harvard University and Loma Linda University in the United States has demonstrated that drinking extra water reduces fatigue and stress and increases stamina and energy to a remarkable degree. It also eliminates false hunger. Yet few of us drink enough.

On average, in a temperate climate – not sweating from exertion or heat – we need about (3.6 litres) 6 pints a day for optimal health, although few of us consume even as much as (1.2 litres) 2 pints. Provided you are not suffering from a kidney or liver disease, keep a large bottle or two of pure, fresh mineral water on your desk and make sure you consume your quota of this clear, delicious health-giving drink.

How Much Is Enough?

Here's how to work it out:

Divide your *current* weight in kilos by 8. If you weigh 58 kilos then 58 divided by 8 equals 7.25 big glasses. Then round the figure upwards to the next glass and there you have it: 8 glasses a day – at least. But remember that is only a base calculation for a cool day. *You will need a lot more during exercise, or on a hot day.* I drink between 3½ and 4½ litres a day all year round.

---

4. Cut the coffee

Quite apart from the negative effects of caffeine – an ingredient not only of coffee but also of tea and many soft drinks – drinking coffee messes up blood sugar. Caffeine, technically known as *trimethyl xanthine*, is a habit-forming drug. It has been shown to be responsible for headache, insomnia, nervousness, anxiety, and that familiar wired mental state which keeps you buzzing for a time intellectually but tends to disconnect you from your instincts. Caffeine gives you a quick lift and the illusion of energy only to let you crash a couple of hours later when you are inclined to reach for more – or for a sticky bun or chocolate – just to keep going.

Black tea also contains tannic acid – an irritant to the digestive system. In high enough concentrations tannic acid is carcinogenic. Even if you have always been a committed 6 to 8 cups a day tea or coffee drinker, after a couple of weeks on good water you will find you don't miss it. Then when you have an occasional cup it becomes a simple pleasure rather than an addiction.

And what about soft drinks? Many colas, squashes and soft drinks also contain caffeine. And they are far too high in sugar. They bring nutritionally empty calories into your body which you can ill afford. A 350g (12oz) can of cola contains 7 teaspoons of sugar – about 40 grammes. Colas are full of chemicals to pollute your body and disrupt your liver's elimination processes.

Here's the good news. Caffeine in small quantities such as are found in *green* tea can be taken by most people – especially since, unlike coffee and black tea, green tea is full of natural anti-oxidants and other goodies.

5. Identify Your Cravings

You can't pretend they just don't exist. As Snoopy says, 'It's hard to keep your mind on a diet when your stomach just sent out for a pizza,' so what can you do? First understand why you have cravings. Many come in the form of a sweet tooth or a cup of coffee. You feel a little tired and need pepping up, so you eat chocolate or drink coffee. An hour or two later you find yourself even more tired and with an even stronger craving. And the cycle goes on as you put yet more strain on your pancreas to regulate your blood sugar and deplete your body of yet more of the important vitamins and minerals.

Then there are the allergy cravings. You *need* a doughnut or an ice cream – and not just one, but several. Food allergies can leave you feeling ravenously hungry even after eating a large meal. If this happens to you, take a step back, and acknowledge your cravings for what they really are. You will not die, nor will you even suffer, without that quick junk food snack, and the sooner you realize it, the better. Explore the food allergy question. You may well be allergic/addicted to the foods you crave – especially wheat, milk or sugar. Real awareness without self-blame will help you take steps to banish cravings permanently.

6. Chuck the Fats

Experiments have shown that when someone eats a meal high in *any* kind of fat, the fats form a film around red blood cells and platelets and encourages them to stick together or clump. This clumping causes small capillaries to clog and even shut down so that as much as 20% of your normal blood circulation is lost, reducing the amount of oxygen available to your cells by about 30%. This clumping and its corresponding oxygen-cell deficit lasts for many hours after eating a meal high in fat. The action of fat on the brain is one of the main reasons why you can feel sleepy or unable to think clearly after eating a heavy meal. Particularly dangerous are processed unsaturated fats found in cooking oils, margarines and convenience foods. Avoid them, and get your fats as they come in nature – in whole grains, pulses, nuts, seeds and avocados. Use small amounts of butter on your toast if you need a spread and extra virgin olive oil on your salads.

7. Sort Your Snacks

The time when you are most likely to confront the junk food impulse is when you decide to 'grab a quick bite to eat' to sustain you between meals, or even to replace a meal. If all you can find for a snack is a chocolate bar or packaged apple pie you are better off going hungry. Missing a snack, or even a meal for that matter, is no terrible sin. On the other hand, if you are hungry, you are hungry. Try to make sure that you have good snacking material at the ready – a piece of fruit or a bag full of crunchy crudités is ideal. A small container of low-fat cottage cheese or even a tin of water-packed tuna is great. Sunflower seeds or unsalted nuts can also be good energy sustainers, but make sure they are really *fresh*, and remember that these foods are also high in fat so you may not want to eat them too frequently.

8. Clear Your Cupboards

You can't tell every fast food restaurant to close down or every street vendor to move his drinks cans out of your sight, but what you can do is be responsible for the food in your own home. Don't take the attitude that since you bought that large chocolate cake you ought to finish it anyway, and don't let it sit around staring you in the face. Get rid of it, or give it away. The sooner you eliminate 'tempting' foods from your own kitchen, the easier it will be for you to forget about them altogether.

9. Steer Clear of Traps

Don't let yourself get into difficult situations socially where you are forced to eat bad foods. Anticipate the junk food traps and be sure to either bring your own foods with you or eat before you go and stir your food around on your plate when you get there. Nobody ever notices. Be determined and don't let obstacles such as cynical remarks from onlookers or 'friends' prevent you from reaching your high energy goals. Actually what you eat and don't eat is none of their business anyway. If the worst comes to the worst and somebody is trying to force

a piece of pie down your throat, thank them but say
sadly, your doctor won't let you eat it because he has
found you are allergic to wheat.

10. Get Moving
One of the easiest ways to lose your dependency on junk
food and to do away with cravings is to get more in touch
with your body through regular exercise. Exercise will
quickly rid your body of metabolic wastes, the presence
of which makes you crave junk foods.

Spring Clean Your Body

Get out your energy workbook and make some notes
about what specific actions you can take in your own life
to junk junk food forever. Then – if you are impatient to
have more energy fast – turn your attention to beginning
the detox process. The simplest and quickest way to help
free yourself of junk-food cravings and instantly boost
your energy is to give your body a good clear out.
Remember how good you feel when you spring clean
your house – how much clearer you feel and how much
energy you suddenly have to start new projects once you
have cleared out the dust and junk of the winter? You
feel even better and will have even more energy once
you have begun to clear the wastes that have accumulat-
ed in your body. There are many ways to do this. Try a
simple detox diet based mostly on raw foods (see
Resources, p. 153 for *10 Day Clean Up Plan*) or simply do
a couple of days on a fruit fast before altering your diet
for good.

Fruit Fasting

In truth the two-day fruit fast is not a fast at all. You eat as
much as you want – but only fruit – in place of your regular meals, and in between too if you like. Fruit fasting is
not for those with Candida albicans or a blood sugar
problem. If you suspect you have either, you need to

detox your body very slowly using the eating plan in Bite into Energy (Step 6), avoiding *any* fruit. Eat lots of vegetables instead.

I would suggest that you choose to fruit fast over a weekend, eating nothing but fruit on Saturday and Sunday, and beginning on the Friday by cutting out all stimulants such as coffee and tea, and all depressants such as alcohol for the day. Also avoid bread and cooked carbohydrates such as pasta and cereals, and make your last meal of the day a large raw salad of vegetables and fruits.

A fruit fast is one of the best ways of clearing your body quickly, but because the effect is so dramatic you may find that you experience some mild elimination reactions such as a headache, irritability or tiredness at some point during the two days. This is why I suggest doing a fruit fast over a weekend so that you can rest and pamper yourself when necessary.

The fruit fast is effective in several ways. In a purely physical sense fruit is mildly laxative and a wonderful intestinal 'broom' to sweep your alimentary canal clean. Also, fruit is alkaline-forming, and most stored wastes are acid in character. When your body is given the chance to throw off these wastes they enter the bloodstream where the alkalinity of the fruit helps to neutralize them so that they can be quickly expelled. This helps minimize the possibility of any cleansing reactions. Fruit also has a high potassium content. This is helpful in ridding the system of excess water and oedema in the tissues, increasing oxygenation in the cells and raising cell vitality.

Cleansing Reactions

It is possible that you may experience one or more cleansing reactions (although many people don't). If you do, there is no need to worry. It is all part of the elimination process. But it is important to acknowledge them. Such reactions can include headaches, muscle or joint

pains, sensitivity, tiredness and unsettled emotions. They
are simply due to the rapid mobilization and release of
stored toxins and wastes. Should they occur it is best to
retire to a quiet, dark room and rest for a while. Also try
to get plenty of fresh air – breathing deeply is another
way of ridding your body of wastes. Beware of overtaxing
your body by strenuous exercise; it is working very hard
to clean and renew itself and therefore just now it
doesn't need added strain.

Fruit Fun

It is up to you to choose the *single* fruit which you intend
to eat throughout the day. Each fruit has its own specific
health-benefiting properties. I have found that apples,
grapes, pineapple, papaya, mango and watermelon are
particularly successful.

- **Apples:** Excellent for detoxification – the pectin in
  apples helps remove impurities from the system.
  Pectin also helps prevent protein matter in the
  intestines from putrefying. The high fibre content of
  apples also makes them great 'brooms'. Apples are
  good for strengthening the liver and digestive system
  and for stimulating body secretions. They are rich in
  vitamins and minerals.
- **Grapes**: Very effective cleansers for the skin, liver,
  intestines and kidneys, due to their potent properties
  which counter excessive mucus in your system. Grapes
  provide a quick source of energy which is easily assimilated and, rich in minerals, they make good blood and
  cell builders.
- **Pineapple**: Has a high concentration of bromelin, an
  enzyme which supports the action of hydrochloric
  acid in your stomach and helps to break down protein
  wastes in the system. Eating pineapple is also believed
  to soothe internal inflammation, accelerate tissue
  repair, regulate the glandular system and clear mucus.

- **Papaya and Mango**: These tropical fruits (mango to a lesser degree) contain an enzyme called papain which resembles the enzyme pepsin in the stomach and, like bromelin, helps to break down protein waste in the tissues. Papaya and mango are good for cleansing the alimentary canal and helping digestive disorders. Mangoes are also believed to relieve depression.

- **Watermelon:** A wonderful diuretic and great for washing your system clean. It is used to ease stomach ulcers and high blood-pressure and to soothe the intestinal tract. Juice the rind of the watermelon with the seeds and a little flesh and drink it about half an hour before a melon meal to get all the benefit of the chlorophyll-rich skin and vitamin-packed seeds.

Eat one fruit only throughout each of the two days because this is less taxing for the digestive system. If, however, the amount of a certain fruit available is limited, you can change fruit mid-day as long as you leave a gap of at least two hours before starting the new fruit. How much fruit you choose to eat is up to you. You will find that you need to eat more frequently than usual as fruit is digested very quickly and does not remain in the stomach for more than an hour. You might want to take about four to five fruit meals spread throughout the day (eating continually is tiring for the digestive system), but should you feel hungry at any point have a fruit snack.

Eat nothing else during this two-day period and do not drink tea or coffee. You may have herb teas such as peppermint, lemon or camomile – with a teaspoon of honey if you wish. And of course, drink lots of spring water.

Enjoy your weekend, make sure that you get some pleasant exercise such as walking, and indulge yourself with reading, listening to music, and plenty of rest. Many people find that their sexuality is heightened during these days. If so, enjoy it. Fruit is great to munch in bed.

Back to Your Workbook

While you are fruit fasting and hopefully getting a little more rest than usual to support the dynamic clear-out process that is going on, turn back to your energy workbook and record whatever symptoms come up as your body cleanses itself. Sometimes these are physical but often as the body cleanses itself you can find yourself experiencing negative feelings too: discouragement, for instance, or anxiety, depression or irritability.

Use your energy workbook to record these feelings without judgement. Just start writing and let the words pour out without stopping your hand and without thinking about what you are writing. Then date the page and just let it go at that. You do not need to analyse any of it. In fact you may never read it again. However, getting such experiences down in words is a powerful way of externalizing some of the potential energy that may have been locked into repressed feelings. (It all works in very much the same way as when a fruit fast brings stored physical wastes to the surface to be eliminated through the skin, the breath, the urine and bowels.) On the other hand you may discover, three or four weeks down the road – when you are feeling more energetic and clearer-minded – that it can be useful to go back and read some of what you have written.

A Record of Change

Making a record can have positive results. Once you have more energy and you are feeling much more positive about everything it can be easy to forget the 'bad times' and assume that life has always been this good. Discovering how much your feelings have changed can reinforce the positive commitments you will have made in recent weeks to energizing your life and make you feel justly proud of the commitment and hard work you have put into your own energy journey. Also, re-reading the outpourings of feelings that can take place when you are spring-cleaning your body and psyche can give you a clear understanding that, like the physical pollutants you may have been carrying around in your system, these negative thought and feeling patterns are not really a part of you despite the fact that you have been carrying them for so long. Finding this out for yourself can help create a new and more positive sense of yourself. This in turn builds your energy levels further in what will soon become the opposite of a vicious circle – a circle of vitality into which you will have tapped and from which you will draw strength. Now let's look at how to use foods for energy.

Bite into Energy

Think how sluggish and sleepy you feel after a big traditional Sunday lunch. It may surprise you to hear that the
amount of energy needed to digest food is even greater
than that which you use when taking strenuous exercise.
In fact your body expends more energy on the digestion
of food than on any other function. When you take in
food your body has to redirect blood (and therefore
energy) away from the brain and other organs towards
the gut where your energy reserves are busy breaking
down your meal. When you eat more food than your
body needs you greatly diminish your energy. You also
build up body pollution, for any food in excess – even
good quality food – has a negative effect on the body.

Shun Convenience Foods

Ready-in-a-minute pre-cooked meals, junk foods, and
even the standard meat-and-two-veg Western meal are all
energy-draining ways to eat. They present your digestive
system with the most difficult of all foods for it to break
down and make use of: a concentrated protein (e.g.
meat) eaten together with a concentrated starch (e.g.
bread or potatoes). Convenience foods and junk foods
are also grossly deficient in essential nutrients, creating
even greater energy burdens on your body.

Separate for Energy

Most people's bodies are not designed for the efficient
digestion of more than one concentrated food in the
stomach at the same time. In the simplest terms you

need an acid medium to digest protein, and an alkaline one to digest starch. Eat concentrated proteins and starches together – fish and chips, bacon sandwiches, meat and potatoes – and neither is properly digested. An awareness of this principle – conscientious food combining – lies at the basis of virtually every tradition of natural healing.

If you want to build energy quickly then begin to separate your concentrated starches from your concentrated proteins, eating each at separate meals. This helps protect your system from a build-up of acid wastes, helps restore metabolic balance, and resolve the energy crisis which takes place when digestion is overtaxed. It will also take any excess weight off most people without ever counting a calorie or going on a slimming diet. And most important of all, it can bring you a whole new kind of energy that can have you looking good and feeling better than ever with each passing week.

Back to Nature

For an abundance of energy, you need not only to separate your foods but also to be conscientious about *what* you eat. Our bodies are not genetically equipped to handle the refined flours, sugars, huge quantities of protein and high concentrations of fat which make up the standard Western fare. Our ancestors did not eat massive quantities of white bread, white sugar, junk fats and pre-packaged, pre-cooked foods. They ate simple, ordinary, wholesome foods – as much of them as they could get. Their diet was low in fat, high in complex carbohydrates and only moderate in protein. This is the way our bodies genetically *expect* to be fed – good, wholesome, comfort foods, whole, simply prepared and eaten as closely as possible to their natural state.

This way of eating for energy is based on what I call *real foods* – leafy and root vegetables, whole grains such as brown rice, rye, barley, millet, quinoa, some pulses, fruits and flesh foods. Such a way of eating is naturally low in fat, refined starches and sugars, moderate in protein, rich in fibre, and high in complex carbohydrates from natural foods. Vegetables and sprouted seeds and grains offer the highest complement of vitamins and minerals, essential fatty acids, easily assimilated top-quality protein, fibre and wholesome carbohydrate found in nature. The health-enhancing properties of living foods have long been tested and eulogized by highly respected European and American physicians – from Gordon Latto and Philip Kilsby in Britain, Max Bircher-Benner in Switzerland and Max Gerson in Germany, to Henry Lindlahr and J. K. Tilden in the United States.

Eat Raw for Energy

Raw Energy Food Combining is far from being just another new diet fad. Raw foods are at the root of a healthy high-energy diet. To gain energy through food combining you need 3 to 4 meals a day of which between 50 and 75% should be foods with a naturally high water content (like fresh fruits and vegetables) rather than foods from which moisture has been removed through drying, baking, cooking and processing.

Fresh, uncooked fruits, vegetables, sprouted seeds, and sprouted grains all contain high levels of a special kind of water – the water found naturally in living cells. This water is invaluable for helping your body to transport nutrients to all your cells and for taking toxic waste and fat away and enhancing overall vitality. This living water is quite different from the stuff that you get out of the tap: water in fresh foods carries electrolytes, vitamins, organic minerals, proteins, enzymes, amino acids, carbohydrates, natural sugars, fatty acids and other nutrients. It helps to boost cell metabolism, create more energy, and makes fat burning possible.

The remainder of your diet should consist of the stamina-enhancing whole grains, vegetables, legumes, eggs, soya foods like tofu and soya milk, fresh fish, meat, poultry or game. Once you have gained all the energy you want you can increase your intake of these heavier foods, although many people find that restricting stamina foods to around 30–40% of their diet keeps them feeling and looking well permanently and preserves long-lasting vitality.

Get into Food Combining

Raw Energy Food Combining uses the well-researched and highly effective 'naturecure' principles of food combining and raw energy eating to achieve spectacular energy enhancement. It will also take excess fat off your body without ever dieting. Hundreds of years of conventional and complementary medical experience has shown that eating a diet high in raw ingredients, while avoiding certain 'poor' combinations of foods, assists digestion and detoxification. This kind of diet brings the body into a more healthy balance, encouraging it to burn off excess fat quickly and efficiently.

So how does it work? Raw Energy Food Combining is based on ten very simple rules that once learned and used on a daily basis will soon give you a new vitality – and a new shape to be proud of. All you have to do is follow them as closely as possible. You do not need willpower; you simply need to follow a healthy diet, in other words one that encourages efficient digestion, natural appetite control and detoxification.

The Raw Energy Food Combining eating plan is designed to ensure that the food you eat is digested as thoroughly as possible, creating the minimum amount of toxic by-products which get stored as excess fat and dampen natural energy.

When your body is functioning at optimum rates – as it will if you follow this eating plan – your appetite will find its natural level, your metabolism begins to work more efficiently and your energy levels steadily rise.

When following a food combining eating plan there are certain guidelines you need to follow:

Ten Keys to Energy

1. Never eat a concentrated starch food with a concentrated protein food at the same meal. To find out which foods fall into these categories take a look at the diagram on pages 100–1.

   Concentrated proteins such as meat, fish, eggs and nuts, and starches such as potatoes, bread, cereals and beans require the body to secrete very different types of enzymes in order to be broken down during digestion. These enzymes in turn require very different chemical environments in which to work effectively. Starch-digesting enzymes need an alkaline environment, while protein-digesting enzymes need the opposite – an acid medium. Eating protein and carbohydrate together can and often does result in incomplete digestion. And inefficient digestion means that toxic by-products end up in our fat cells, leading to fatigue, food allergies, cravings, mood swings and weight gain in most people. To make sure that your diet is balanced, try to eat one carbohydrate- and one protein-based meal a day.

2. Breakfast should always consist of only fruit or raw vegetables. Your liver – the body's most important organ for detoxification – is at its most efficient between midnight and midday. Eating only fruit (which is virtually self-digesting) or drinking fruit or vegetable juice for the first half of the day allows the liver to carry on deep cleansing and fat shedding at an optimum rate. All other foods will interfere with this process. Eating fruit or drinking fruit juices with other foods can lead to fermentation in the gut, causing indigestion, wind and discomfort; so if later on in the day you really must eat fruit with other foods, then eat it as a starter rather than at the end

of a meal and be sure to leave at least 20 minutes for its digestion before starting your second course.

3. Eat a large, raw salad at least once a day. This is the best possible way of enabling your body to rebalance and rebuild itself, restoring metabolism to its peak level.

4. Choose high-quality food. Always make sure that you buy the freshest foods and choose whole-grain, unprocessed varieties of everything whenever possible.

5. Make staples your side dishes. Staple foods include meat, poultry, dairy products, fish, legumes, whole grains and cooked vegetables. They are delicious and satisfying and you need them for sustained energy and protein – but use them in moderation. The best way to do this is to serve them as side dishes: think of them as condiments to your raw salads and vegetable meals.

6. Eat lots of 'high-water' foods. Your body is 70% water. For it to detoxify itself and restore normal cell function, 50–75% of your daily diet needs to be made up of high-water foods: i.e. fresh fruit and vegetables – eaten raw. Remember high-water foods bring energy. This is probably one of the easiest guidelines to keep. If you are having only fruit for breakfast and at least one big salad a day, it just about takes care of itself. If you find that you have eaten more staple foods than you should have on any particular day, try to eat nothing but raw foods on the following one to compensate.

7. Don't eat between meals. If you are truly hungry have a piece of fruit or some crunchy raw vegetables. Your system must have time to complete the digestion of a meal before you put anything else into it. Four or five hours need to elapse between lunch and dinner, otherwise digestion will be incomplete, which can cause toxicity and stop you losing weight.

8. Drink plenty of water, up to 4 or 5 litres a day if you can. It brings great energy. Avoid coffee, tea, fizzy drinks and alcohol while on your diet – they are all high in toxins and will hamper the energy-building process. Instead, drink plenty of filtered or mineral water and take advantage of the huge number of delicious herbal teas available.

9. Be creative. My recipes and meal suggestions are merely guidelines. Adjust them to your own tastes and eating styles. Incorporate your favourite foods into your meals. Have fun.

10. Make time for exercise. No matter what mountains you have to move to do it, make sure that you set aside time and space to do at least 30 minutes of exercise four times a week. Try some brisk walking, cycling or swimming – anything that gets your heart rate up. Regular exercise spurs the release of toxicity, boosts the metabolism, firms the body and improves your ability to handle all kinds of stress.

You Can Feel Even Better

If your first response to this advice is to say 'How ridiculous. I have been eating meat and potatoes for years and done perfectly well on it!' think again. If you are completely honest you will probably admit to any number of minor digestive problems, from indigestion and flatulence to persistent hunger and being overweight – not to mention more serious rheumatoid conditions and other chronic ailments. All these problems can develop as a result of subjecting the digestive system to the strain of digesting concentrated starches and proteins at the same meal – something that you *must* avoid if you want to gain more energy.

One last word – and it is an important one. Always consult your doctor before undertaking a change in diet if you think you may have a health problem of any kind. This diet is not designed to replace any diets recommended by your doctor or health professional.

Well Tried and Tested

Raw Energy Food Combining has been used for years to improve health and reduce fatigue. It also offers a permanent solution to digestive problems and can put a stop to out-of-control eating habits – *naturally*.

If you have been eating irregularly, or more than your body needs, or relying on lots of processed foods, your appetite and digestive system will have become distorted. The digestive system of a person who lives on refined foods or who chronically overeats simply does not function normally because it remains in a state of persistent stimulation. As a result, good digestion is impaired and nutritional deficiencies can occur. Many people in this state go on to experience chronic fatigue or hunger and food cravings as the body calls out for adequate supplies of essential vitamins and minerals. Another consequence of poor eating habits is a metabolic slowdown, triggered again by poor digestion. When this happens energy levels sink and you gain weight easily.

Goodbye to Food Addictions

Food sensitivities frequently contribute to a sense of fatigue and can be an important cause of excess weight. The woman who reaches for a biscuit to go with her cup of tea but who ends up eating the whole packet may not know it but she is experiencing symptoms of the allergy-addiction which forms the basis of food sensitivities. As I have explained, people often develop cravings for foods to which they are mildly allergic. Their food sensitivities over-stimulate the digestive system so that it produces too many juices, which leads to persistent hunger. This in turn is translated into over-eating. For instance, if the woman eating the biscuit has a mild allergy to wheat, the snack will trigger too much digestive juice which leads to a craving for more food.

Consuming foods to which you are sensitive also creates excess levels of toxic waste – far more than your lymphatic system and liver can efficiently eliminate, and this depletes you of vitality. If you have a tendency to gain weight your body lays down even more protective fat to lock these toxins out of harm's way. If not, the toxicity tends to build up and predispose you to degenerative disease and early ageing. Raw Energy Food Combining is the antidote to all of these problems.

- It gradually eliminates cravings by supplying your body with the nutrients it needs to function at its optimum level.
- The high quantity of raw foods you will be eating calms down an irritated and over-active digestive system so that its functions can gradually return to normal and eliminate hunger symptoms.
- A raw energy way of eating brings high energy and natural appetite control. Improvements in digestion and weight loss take place steadily and naturally, without having to pay attention to either.
- Skin and muscles become firmer and the whole body undergoes a process of regeneration and rejuvenation.

Let's look at what to eat:

Fruit or Raw Vegetable Breakfasts

A beautifully simple and essential part of the diet, your Raw Energy Food Combining breakfast should consist of nothing but fresh fruit or fresh raw vegetables. They are best eaten on an empty stomach as their vitamins and minerals are absorbed into the bloodstream almost immediately.

- Eat as much as you like – up to 1lb at a time – but make sure you chew very thoroughly.
- If you get hungry mid-morning have another piece or two of fruit.
- Steer clear of dried fruit until you have lost all the excess weight you want to lose.

- Eat bananas only if they are very ripe and you feel that you need a heavier food. Leave 45 minutes before you have your lunch.

- *Forget fruit and eat only vegetables if you have a blood sugar or candida problem.*

- Never over-eat – but likewise never under-eat. Have just as much as you need to feel satisfied. You could try one of these fruit recipes, which can also be eaten as a light supper or energizing lunch. Here are some good fruit breakfasts:

  o **Pear Supreme**: Slice four unpeeled pears and lay slices out in a dish. Mix together 2 tbsp runny honey, the juice of two lemons and three drops of oil of peppermint in a glass and pour over the pear. Chill in a refrigerator for 30 minutes and garnish with half a cup of fresh blackcurrants just before serving.

  o **Live Apple Sauce**: Core and chop four apples and liquidize with enough apple juice to make a medium thick sauce. Add a dash of cinnamon or nutmeg and a little honey to sweeten. Serve immediately. (Add 100g (4oz) chopped pecans for a nutritious all-fruit meal later in the day.)

  o **Tropical Delight**: Peel, slice and deseed a papaya. Place in a bowl with two chopped, ripe bananas and a peeled and diced mango. Pour a quarter of a cup of apple juice over the fruit and serve immediately, garnished with nutmeg. (Add 2 tbsp coconut to make this an all-fruit lunch or supper.)

  o **Exotic Apricot Frappé**: Put 4–5 pitted fresh apricots into a blender with the juice of two small oranges, a pinch of coriander and a small handful of ice and whizz until liquid.

  o **Apple Raspberry Frappé**: Core and chop (but don't peel) two sweet apples. Place in a blender with half a teaspoon of finely chopped lemon balm or mint, quarter of a cup of fresh raspberries, a little spring water (and a small handful of ice cubes if you want a chilled drink). Blend thoroughly.

The Vegetable Choice

I personally prefer fresh pressed vegetable juices for breakfast. I especially like carrot with beetroot and some green leaves of dandelion, lettuce, or spinach from the garden. More often, however, my breakfast consists of a glass of spring water into which I have stirred a heaped tablespoon of Pure Synergy which I find gives me greater support for sustained energy than anything I have ever eaten (see Resources, page 149). To this I add a handful of green leaves.

If you have been used to a diet of convenience foods, however, you will probably want to begin slowly to intro-duce yourself to the *green foods* – whether this be by adding a handful of dandelion leaves, lettuce, or spinach to your energy drink or spooning in some powdered spir-ulina, green barley, or Pure Synergy. Green foods (about which we'll find out more in the next chapter) are about as far away from convenience foods as you can get and for some people they take a little getting used to. The first green drink you make you may only add a leaf or two of a green vegetable or as little as half a teaspoon of powdered green superfoods to a glass of fresh fruit or vegetable juice. Give yourself time to get used to the green flavours. As your body detoxifies you will not only find the greens easier to take – you are likely to end up loving them. When this happens you can use as much as 100g (4oz) of green leaf herbs and vegetables in a big glass of fresh fruit or vegetable juice or a heaped table-spoon of powdered green superfoods.

Make a Great Salad

To most people a salad is a pleasant side dish used to set off a main course. With Raw Energy Food Combining everything is turned around. All the salads here should be used as the mainstay of an individual meal. They can be served on their own for lunch or dinner as a neutral meal (neither protein nor carbohydrate-based). Or they can be combined with either a protein sidedish (nuts, fish, tofu, meat or eggs are good choices) to create a protein meal or a starchy sidedish (wholemeal bread – preferably 100% rye – crispbreads, a baked potato, a vegetable rice dish, couscous or legumes like kidney or butter beans) to create a starch meal. But, remember, under no circumstances should you eat protein and starch at the *same* meal. Always choose only the freshest vegetables. Cucumbers, celery and sweet peppers should be firm to the touch. Ingredients such as carrots and broccoli should be snappy and crisp. Cut all the ingredients into bite-size pieces, except for lettuces and greens which should be left as leaves or torn into smaller shreds.

- **Devil's Delight** (neutral): Put 2 tbsp olive oil, 1 tbsp lemon juice, 1 tbsp Meaux mustard, 3 tbsp chopped parsley, 4 chopped spring onions, finely ground black pepper to taste and 1 tbsp vegetable bouillon in a screw-top jar and shake. Pour dressing over salad and toss all the ingredients together.

- **Green Glory** (neutral): Place 250g (8oz) shredded Chinese leaves, 1 chopped green pepper, 3 tbsp finely chopped fresh mint, 4 sticks chopped celery and 3 sliced spring onions in a bowl. Shake 4 tbsp mayonnaise, 2 tbsp orange juice, grated rind of half an orange, 2 tbsp fresh chopped parsley, 1 tsp sea salt and 2 cloves finely chopped garlic in a screw-top jar and dress salad. Add chopped boiled eggs or strips of vegetable omelette for a protein meal or baked potato to make a starch meal.

- **Jerusalem Artichoke Salad** (neutral): Mix together 6 grated Jerusalem artichokes with 3 grated carrots, a finely chopped apple, 3 tbsp finely chopped parsley, 3 sticks of chopped celery and 3 handfuls of Chinese leaves, chopped. Dress with a mixture of olive oil, lemon juice, a little mustard, Worcester sauce, cayenne pepper and crushed garlic. Sprinkle with pumpkin or sunflower seeds for protein. Serve with pumpernickel bread for a starchy option.

- **Root-is-Best Salad** (neutral): Mix together 2 finely grated turnips, 3 grated parsnips, 2 grated carrots, 3 chopped spring onions, half a green and half a red pepper (chopped) and 1 tbsp chopped savory or lovage. Pour the juice of 1 lemon over the salad. Toss and serve on a bed of grated Chinese leaves or lettuce. Serve with grated hard-boiled egg or a good quality mayonnaise for protein or add toasted rye bread for a starch meal option.

- **Watercress Salad** (neutral): Mix together 3 handfuls of Cos lettuce, a bunch of chopped watercress, 4 chopped spring onions, 3 large courgettes (grated), 2 grated carrots and 4 quartered tomatoes. Make a light vinaigrette by blending 2 tbsp cider vinegar with 4 tbsp olive oil, half a teaspoon Meaux mustard, half a teaspoon tarragon, half a teaspoon chervil and half a teaspoon sea salt. Add a small tin of tuna in brine or sprinkle over 3–4 tbsp of sunflower seeds for a tasty protein dish. Serve with buckwheat or steamed brown rice for a starch meal.

Most of the salad recipes above are quite elaborate, but you can always make up your own to suit your individual taste, as long as you stick to mixing salad vegetables with either proteins (tuna fish, egg, cold chicken, or red kidney beans) or carbohydrates (baked potato, toasted rye bread, rice or buckwheat cooked with spicy vegetable stock).

However, you can try a deliciously quick and simple neutral alternative by using this classic salad formula: take a grated root vegetable such as a carrot, parsnip or turnip and combine it with an equal amount of a leafy vegetable such as watercress, lamb's lettuce or Chinese leaf and a bulb vegetable such as red or green pepper.

Use the salad dressing of your choice taken from any of the recipes above to flavour the salad and add a protein or starch element (which you can also pick at random from any of the recipes) as you require.

Tasty Toppings

The following protein-based dressings can be poured over salad or steamed vegetables to make a delicious lunch or dinner or used as a dip with crudités.

- **Nut Mayonnaise** (protein): In a blender or food processor blend 100g (4oz) cashew nuts with a teacup of spring water, 2 cloves of chopped garlic, the juice of a lemon, 1 tsp vegetable bouillon (see Resources, p. 151) or tamari and 3 finely chopped spring onions. Chill and serve. (Will keep for four days in the fridge.)

- **Pink Tofu Dressing** (protein): Mix together 1 teacup of tofu, 4 tbsp tomato purée, 1 tsp Meaux mustard, half a clove finely chopped garlic and half a teaspoon vegetable bouillon powder. Add 1 tbsp chopped shallots and mix again. Serve chilled. (Will keep for five days in the fridge.)

- **Raw Hummus** (protein): Put 2 big teacups of sprouted chickpeas (sprouted for 2 or 3 days), a chopped clove of garlic, 3 tbsp tahini (sesame seed paste), the juice of three lemons, 2 tbsp tamari and enough water to thin the mixture into a blender or food processor. Blend thoroughly, then mix in 3 tsp chopped spring onions or chives and chill. (Will keep for 2 or 3 days in the fridge.)

Energy Soups

- **Yummy Avocado and Tomato** (neutral): Blend 6 ripe tomatoes, a ripe avocado, 2 finely chopped spring onions, quarter of a teaspoon dill seed, a pinch of cayenne, 300ml (1/2 pint) spring water, 2 tsp vegetable bouillon powder and 1 tsp kelp (optional). Add 2 finely chopped tomatoes and a raw, finely chopped green pepper. Serve hot or cold, with wholemeal bread for a carbohydrate meal or topped with chopped, grilled bacon for a protein alternative.

- **Chilled Cucumber Soup** (protein): Blend a large, chopped cucumber with 2 cups of soya milk and a few ice cubes. Add 2 tsp vegetable bouillon powder and continue to blend. Then add 4 tbsp chopped mint, blend briefly and serve immediately, topped with crushed poppy seeds.

- **Corn Soup** (starch): Wash 2 fresh corn cobs and cut the kernels off the cob. Mix the corn with 300ml (1/2 pint) *warm* spring water, 2 chopped spring onions, 1 tsp olive oil and 1 tsp vegetable bouillon powder or sea salt. Season with tahini (sesame seed paste) if desired, and blend until creamy.

Lunch or Dinner Recipes

Leave at least four to five hours between lunch and dinner for efficient digestion. Do not snack unless a meal is going to be delayed and it is more than four or five hours since you have eaten, in which case you can have a little fruit or a few raw vegetables. Eat as much as you need, depending on how hungry you are. Take your time, chew thoroughly and stop as soon as you feel you have had enough. Do not overeat.

Most of the recipes given will feed four, but on this diet you can actually eat as much as you like, as long as you listen to your appetite. All you have to remember is to chew your food slowly and thoroughly and stop eating as soon as your appetite signals that you have had enough. Do not overeat: that saps energy faster than anything.

Super Stir-Fries

These attractive and marvellously quick meals are based on the Chinese principle of frying foods very quickly in a minute quantity of light oil to preserve texture and vitamins. They are easy to prepare. Simply chop all your ingredients finely so they cook in around three minutes.

And don't be afraid to create your own combinations – just make sure that you don't mix carbohydrates and proteins in the same dish.

- **Green Salmon Stir-fry** (protein): Heat 1 tbsp soya oil or extra virgin olive oil in a wok or large frying pan. Stir-fry 125g (4oz) fresh salmon cut into strips with 2 cloves of finely chopped garlic for 2 minutes. Add 225g (8oz) Chinese leaves, 225g (8oz) broccoli florets and 225g (8oz) green beans, all finely chopped, and stir-fry for a further 4 minutes. Add 1 tbsp vegetable or fish stock to the juice of 1 lemon, pour over the ingredients, stir in well and serve immediately with a watercress salad.

- **Sesame and Courgette Stir-Fry** (protein): Cut 225g (8oz) courgettes, 8 sticks of celery and 225g (8oz) carrots into match-sticks. Heat 2 tsp soya or olive oil in a wok or frying pan. Add 125g (4oz) sesame seeds and cook for 1–2 minutes until they start to brown. Add the vegetables and cook for another 2–3 minutes. Season with soy sauce or tamari and serve.

- **Ultra-High Stir-Fry** (neutral): Heat 2 tsp of soya oil or olive oil in a wok or large frying pan. Stir-fry 225g (8oz) bean sprouts and a large, thinly sliced red pepper for 2 minutes. Add soy sauce to taste, season with black pepper and serve. Add thin strips of pork or chicken to create a satisfying protein meal, or serve with fine noodles for a carbohydrate option.

- **Mangetout and Almond Stir-Fry** (protein): (Replace almonds with finely-sliced chicken or prawns if desired.) Top and tail 225g (8oz) of mangetout. Heat 2 tsp soya oil in a wok or large frying pan. When hot, add 50g (2oz) blanched almonds and stir-fry for three minutes. Add the mangetout, 125g (4oz) button mushrooms and soy sauce to taste. Serve immediately.

- **Spicy Shish Kebab** (neutral): This is a delicious, marinated vegetable dish that you can grill or barbecue. You can serve it on a bed of brown rice, buckwheat or quinoa, that has been cooked in bouillon powder with a little chilli or tamari to make a satisfying meal. Alternatively you can cut down on the vegetables and add 450g (1lb) of lamb or chicken chunks to the marinade and cook on the skewers for a delicious protein option.

Make a marinade in a large bowl by mixing together 1¼ teacups of olive oil, the juice of 3 lemons, 2 tbsp finely chopped parsley, half a teaspoon ground nutmeg, 1 tbsp chopped fresh basil and 1 tsp dried oregano. Add 1 large aubergine cut into 3cm (1¼ in) chunks, 10 halved fresh tomatoes, 24 large mushrooms, 1 red pepper, 1 green pepper, and 2 large red onions, all cut into chunks. Let it stand for three hours. Skewer the ingredients alternately and use the remaining marinade to baste them as they are grilled or barbecued.

- **Baked Leeks and Chicken** (protein): You can turn this into a carbohydrate meal by leaving out the chicken and replacing it with garlic croûtons made by frying 125g (4oz) whole rye bread cut into tiny squares in a little olive oil flavoured with garlic.

  Slice 450g (1lb) leeks lengthways into very fine strips and then cut into 8cm (3 in) lengths. Mix with 1 tbsp olive oil and bake in a hot oven for 10–15 minutes. Meanwhile, finely chop 125g (4oz) chicken and brown lightly in a non-stick pan. When the chicken is almost crispy, add 1 tbsp fresh chopped parsley, a splash of water and salt and pepper. Pour over the leeks and serve.

- **Polenta** (starch): This peasant dish made from corn-meal is delicious with a salad dressed in a spicy sauce. Heat 450ml (¾ pint) water in a kettle. Pour the boiling water into the saucepan over a teacupful of polenta corn-meal seasoned with a little sea salt. Stir until smooth and then cook very gently until all the liquid has been absorbed. Cool and drop by the spoonful onto a lightly oiled baking sheet. Grill until brown, turning once.

The Special Foods

To make eating more exciting make the most of some of the more unusual ingredients available from larger supermarket branches and healthfood shops.

Sea Vegetables: Available in oriental food shops and healthfood stores, sea vegetables impart a wonderful spicy flavour to soups and salads. They are also the richest natural source of organic mineral salts and are particularly beneficial for the proper functioning of the thyroid gland. You can use powdered kelp as a seasoning as you would salt and pepper. Nori – a seaweed that comes in long thin strips – is a delicious snack food, raw or toasted. The other sea vegetables such as dulse, arame and wakami need to be soaked for a few minutes in tepid water before being chopped and added to raw salads or soups.

Sprouts: Bean and seed sprouts make tasty additions to your weight-loss programme. Sprouted foods supply unique combinations of enzymes, minerals and vitamins. Try alfalfa seeds, adzuki beans, mung beans, lentils, fenugreek seeds, radish seeds, buckwheat, flax, mint and red clover. You can buy them sprouted or sprout them yourself in jam jars in the kitchen.

Nuts and Seeds: Rich sources of body-building protein and essential fatty acids, nuts and seeds should be eaten regularly as part of your diet but never in great quantities. It's also a good idea not to combine them with any other concentrated food in the same meal. Try almonds, brazils, caraway seeds, cashews, coconut, hazelnuts, pecans, pine kernels, pumpkin seeds, sesame seeds, sunflower seeds or walnuts.

Juices: With a centrifugal juicer you can make some highly nutritious raw energy drinks from fresh vegetables and fruits. If you don't have a juicer, there are also a number of high quality juices on the market that are worth looking out for. Go for those that have been processed at a low heat.

How to Cope with Eating Out

What about special circumstances? How can you make
the Raw Energy Food Combining diet work for you when
you have to eat out at a restaurant, when you are travelling, or when you want to take a packed lunch to work?
It's easy.

- **In a restaurant:** Most restaurants serve decent salads –
  a vital part of eating for energy. If you want to eat a
  protein-based fish, meat or game dish with your salad,
  then order something which is simply prepared and
  definitely not smothered in starchy breadcrumbs or
  batter. If your protein dish comes with rice or
  potatoes, ask the waiter if you can have a selection of
  vegetables instead. And avoid the bread basket at all
  costs. If you want to eat carbohydrates with your salad,
  then choose something like a pasta with a vegetable
  or tomato-based sauce – not protein-rich cream or
  cheese. Most restaurants also offer herbal teas at
  the end of the meal, but carry your own just in case.
  And by all means enjoy a glass of good wine occasionally.

- **Flying, or travelling by train or car:** This is the ideal
  time to spend a day on a detox fruit fast. It will help
  your stamina and ability to withstand stress. Simply
  take a bag of fresh fruit or crunchy vegetables with you
  to munch on. Or do as I do and drink masses of spring
  water on a flight with a tablespoon of Pure Synergy
  stirred into it. If you don't want to fast you can usually
  pre-order a healthy vegetarian meal (with 24 hours'
  notice).

- **Packed lunches:** Raw vegetables and fruits are quick
  to prepare and make excellent lunch-box fillers.
  Combine a selection of delicious crudités with a
  protein-rich seed or nut dip or spicy mayonnaise.
  Alternatively, if you have got a busy day ahead and
  need extra energy, take some freshly baked wholemeal

bread (preferably whole rye bread) spread with Marmite or a mashed avocado, plus a fresh salad dressed in vinaigrette.

Ten Keys to Energy – Checklist

1. Never eat a concentrated starch (bread, potatoes, beans or rice) with a conentrated protein (meat, fish, eggs or nuts) at the same meal. But have at least one carbohydrate- and one protein-based meal a day.

2. Eat only fresh fruit or fresh raw vegetables and their juices for breakfast. This allows deep cleansing and permits the liver to function as efficiently as possible.

3. Have a large, raw salad (which rates as neutral food and can happily be combined with either a starch or a protein food) at least once a day.

4. Choose high-quality food – fresh, whole and unprocessed.

5. Make staples – meat, poultry, eggs, legumes, and whole grains – side dishes (no more than 25% of your daily diet) to raw salad and vegetable meals.

6. Eat lots of 'high-water' foods – especially raw vegetables. Your body is 70% water, so for it to detoxify itself and restore normal cell function, 50–75% of your daily diet needs to be made up of high-water foods.

7. Don't eat between meals, except for a little fruit or a glass of freshly made vegetable juice if you are truly hungry.

8. Avoid coffee, tea and alcohol. They are all high in toxins and will put a damper on your energy. Drink lots of filtered or mineral water.

9. Be creative. Adjust the recipes to your tastes and incorporate your favourite foods.

10. Make time for exercise – try to get at least 30 minutes 3–4 times a week.

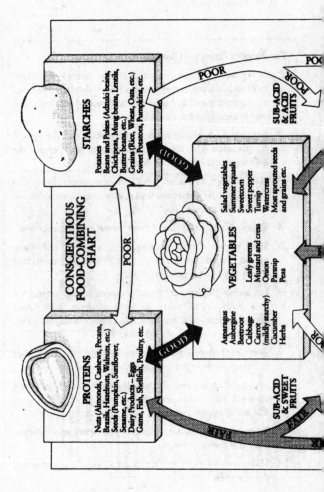

CONSCIENTIOUS FOOD-COMBINING CHART

STARCHES
Potatoes
Beans and Pulses (Adzuki beans, Chickpeas, Mung beans, Lentils, Butter beans, etc.)
Grains (Rice, Wheat, Oats, etc.)
Sweet Potatoes, Pumpkin, etc.

PROTEINS
Nuts (Almonds, Cashews, Pecans, Brazils, Hazelnuts, Walnuts, etc.)
Seeds (Pumpkin, Sunflower, Sesame, etc.)
Dairy Products – Eggs
Game, Fish, Shellfish, Poultry, etc.

VEGETABLES

Asparagus
Aubergine
Beetroot
Cabbage
Carrot (mildly starchy)
Cucumber
Herbs

Leafy greens
Mustard and cress
Onion
Parsnip
Peas

Salad vegetables
Summer squash
Sweetcorn
Sweet pepper
Turnip
Watercress
Most sprouted seeds and grains etc.

SUB-ACID & ACID FRUITS

SUB-ACID & SWEET FRUITS

POOR

POOR

GOOD

POOR

GOOD

GOOD

FAIR

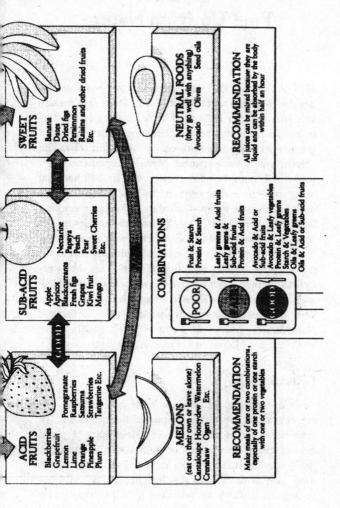

SWEET FRUITS

Banana
Dates
Dried figs
Persimmon
Raisins and other dried fruits
Etc.

NEUTRAL FOODS
(they go well with anything)

Avocado   Olives   Seed oils

RECOMMENDATION

All juices can be mixed because they are
liquid and can be absorbed by the body
within half an hour

SUB-ACID FRUITS

Apple
Apricot
Blackcurrants
Fresh figs
Grapes
Kiwi fruit
Mango

Nectarine
Papaya
Peach
Pear
Sweet Cherries
Etc.

COMBINATIONS

POOR — Fruit & Starch
Protein & Starch

FAIR — Leafy greens & Acid fruits
Leafy greens &
Sub-acid fruits
Protein & Acid fruits

GOOD — Avocado & Acid or
Sub-acid fruits
Avocado & Leafy vegetables
Protein & Leafy greens
Starch & Vegetables
Oils & Leafy greens
Oils & Acid or Sub-acid fruits

ACID FRUITS

Blackberries
Grapefruit
Lemon
Lime
Orange
Pineapple
Plum

Pomegranate
Raspberries
Satsuma
Strawberries
Tangerine Etc.

MELONS
(eat on their own or leave alone)

Cantaloupe Honeydew Watermelon
Crenshaw Ogen Etc.

RECOMMENDATION

Make meals of one or two combinations,
especially of one protein or one starch
with one or two vegetables

GOOD

Step Seven
Fuel Up from Nature

The old adage 'Eat your greens if you want to stay healthy' is now scientific fact. Green foods fuel sustainable energy better than other kinds. And the fun of it all is that so far advanced nutritional scientists know that green works wonders but nobody is yet sure why. The chlorophyll? The enzymes? Mystery ingredients? Yes, probably, but maybe other reasons too. You will find that many of the leading-edge nutritional energy supplements have gone green – spirulina, chlorella, green barley, blue-green algae. Why? Because the nutrients they contain – from vitamins and minerals to trace elements, phytohormones, plant anti-oxidants, enzymes and as yet unidentified health-promoting factors – are not only richest in green foods but are found there in perfect balance and synergy as well as in a highly bioavailable form. Your system just laps them up. Meanwhile herbs and plant factors – facets of Nature's green world – have much to offer when it comes to energy enhancement.

Grass Secrets

Some of the most useful green foods for energy are the cereal grasses. They are also some of the least known. In dried form, a teaspoon or more of dried juice of cereal grasses stirred into a glass of fresh vegetable juice can really spike it up. Taken in capsule form they can be used daily as nutritional supplements. In ancient times young cereal plants were treated with the respect they deserve. Tiny green tips of baby wheat plants were eaten as a delicacy in the Holy Land 2,000 years ago. Then in the 1920s and 1930s in the United States – before vitamin and mineral pills were in existence – bottled, dehydrated cereal grasses were for a time a popular food supplement. With the advent of synthetic vitamins they were almost forgotten, but in the last ten or fifteen years the consumption of young grasses – wheat or rye or oat or barley – has begun to rise.

Young grasses are very different from the mature grains they eventually turn into and from which we make our breads and porridge. When rice, wheat, corn, oats, barley, rye, or millet are planted in good healthy soil, given plenty of rain, and then harvested at exactly the right moment, not only do they taste sweet but they are unbelievably rich in energy-giving vitamins and minerals, enzymes and growth hormones. They are *living foods* – and the juice pressed from them carries these life energies into your body. A young germinated plant is a little miracle of nature. In its tiny leaves photosynthesis produces simple sugars which it transforms into proteins, fatty acids and nucleic acids such as DNA and RNA as well as complex carbohydrates, thanks to the work of enzymes and substrates produced from minerals provided by the soil.

Quantum Energy

One energy-promoting ingredient in young cereal grasses and green foods which has been well established is chlorophyll – the stuff that makes plants green. The chlorophyll molecule is unique in the universe. It is the only substance which has the ability to convert the energy of the sun into chemical energy through the mysterious process of photosynthesis. It is thanks to the chlorophyll molecule that plants make carbohydrates out of carbon dioxide and water. All of life on earth draws its power to be from the sun's energy thanks to photosynthesis in plants. After more than 75 years of research most scientists have come to believe that it is probably the synergistic effect of the chlorophyll and the vital nutrients – both known and unknown – found together with it in the plants from which it comes that has such a positive impact on human health. These nutrients include iron, copper, calcium, magnesium, pyridoxine, folic acid and vitamins C, B12, K and A. Wouldn't you like to tap into the sun's energy?

Pick Your Weeds

Some of the very best of the green foods for energy are the weeds – plants that grow wild in your garden or in fields and hedgerows in the countryside. Dandelion, nettles, ragweed and lamb's quarter are especially good sources of the minerals that our bodies lack as a result of chemical farming which has removed them from the subsoil. This is especially important when it comes to trace elements. Plants such as nettles only grow on mineral-rich soils. Weeds are deep feeders. They are capable of absorbing through their root systems all sorts of goodness that crops cultivated on depleted soils have no access to and they store up valuable nutrients in a wonderful, easily digestible balance. A handful of young nettles (they don't sting yet) is a great boon to a glass of carrot and apple juice. Lamb's quarter, a wayside spring and summer plant, is not only rich in minerals, thanks to being a particularly 'deep diver', it also tastes delicious and can be used in salads without ever imparting too heavy a green flavour to what you are making.

Replenish Your Minerals

Seaweeds are full of trace elements that are essential to the body – but in minute quantities. When boron, chromium, cobalt, calcium, iodine, magnesium, manganese, molybdenum, phosphorus, potassium, silicon, silver and sulphur (to mention only a few elements!) are not present the body's metabolism can experience big problems. Unlike the chalk which is added to bread to 'enrich' it with calcium, and most of the mineral supplements you buy in pill form in stores, the minerals in green plants are organic, which means that your body can easily make use of them to build energy. Adding seaweeds such as nori, dulse, kombu, wakami and arame to your soups, salads, casseroles and other foods will gradually restore optimal levels of vital minerals and trace elements to your body. Then the energy-producing enzymes will work as they should and you will be able to experience far greater vitality.

Magic Algae

Queen of all the green foods is spirulina. A near-microscopic form of blue-green fresh water algae, spirulina is one of the finest green foods that you will ever find. Spirulina is probably the single most important nutritional supplement you can use to support energy at the very highest level. It has a superior amino acid profile, and is unusual in that its protein is alkaline-forming in the body rather than acid-forming. This can be very important for detoxifying the system and also for helping you deal with high levels of stress, for the by-products of prolonged stress tend to be acid in character. Spirulina is also rich in vitamins E, B12, C, B1, B5 and B6 as well as beta-carotene and the minerals zinc, copper, manganese and selenium. It also contains good levels of the anti-ageing, anti-oxidant sulphur amino acid *methionine* and *phycocyanin* – a blue pigment structurally similar to beta-carotene which experiments have shown to enhance immune functions. Finally it is rich in important essential fatty acids, although very low in fat. Add from a teaspoon to a tablespoon to a glass of fresh juice or broth.

Balance Your Energies

Chlorella, sometimes called the emerald food, is another green algae with pretty amazing energy-enhancing properties. It gets its name from its high content of chlorophyll – the highest of any known plant. In addition it is rich in vitamins, minerals, fibre, nucleic acids, amino acids, enzymes, something called CGF – chlorella growth factor – and other important compounds. Among the green foods, chlorella is known as the great normalizer, thanks to its apparent ability to alter bodily processes that are under- or over-active so that they return to normal. About 60% of chlorella is protein. The vitamins it contains in good quantity include vitamin C, beta-carotene and other carotenoids, thiamine, riboflavin, pyridoxine, niacin, pantothenic acid, folic acid, vitamin B12, biotin, choline, vitamin K, inositol and PABA. In addition it is rich in minerals and trace elements including phosphorus, potassium, magnesium, sulphur, iron, calcium, manganese, copper, zinc and cobalt. Meanwhile it helps protect the liver from toxic injury so effectively that some practitioners who use it claim it can even help prevent hangovers by promoting the removal of the alcohol from the body.

Quick Energy Greens

When it comes to boosting energy temporarily, other plants have much to offer. Some, such as green tea and guarana, are quick fixers. They can be great for supporting your energy through jet lag. Green tea (*Camellia sinensis*) comes from the same plant as the black tea which we drink in the West. The difference is that where black tea has been allowed to ferment during which the plant's *polyphenols* – potent and beneficial anti-oxidant compounds – are turned into tannins, the leaves of green tea have been steamed to prevent fermentation from taking place and protect its polyphenol content. Green tea contains a small amount of caffeine – 20 to 30 milligrams per cup compared to 150mg in a cup of coffee – which supports energy temporarily. But it also offers much long term, thanks to its polyphenol content. In addition to being really good anti-oxidants, polyphenols are known for their ability to discourage the formation of cancer-causing compounds that we all take in through our foods. The widespread drinking of green tea is now believed to be the reason why rates of cancer in the Orient are so low compared with those in the West. If you feel you still need the odd boost from caffeine, try changing over from your usual cups of tea or coffee to drinking green tea. Once you get used to its taste you may well enjoy it. Certainly your body will.

Brazilian Cocoa Charge

Guarana (*Paullinia sorbilis*) is often called Brazilian cocoa. In South America it comes in sausage-shaped rolls several centimetres long made from a paste of roasted seeds that have been beaten and dried. Guarana is a popular stimulant in South America where people grate some of these rolls into their hands and then swallow the pieces, washing them down with water. In shops these days you can buy guarana either in dried form in capsules, or in a kind of tonic which tastes good. Guarana, like green tea, contains caffeine in relatively small quantities compared with coffee. It is often useful when you need extra energy but is not something you should rely on until your general energy levels have been restored. Guarana has mild diuretic actions and is often useful for people who suffer from rheumatic pains or lumbago. I sometimes also use it to help prevent jet lag.

Make Way for Immune Support

When it comes to restoring energy long term, look to some of the immune-supporting plant friends such as shiitake mushrooms, golden seal and echinacea. These natural wonders all contain specific immune-supporting and immune-enhancing elements that can, together with your new energy-orientated lifestyle, help rebuild your body and your vitality. Shiitake mushrooms, like their cousins reishi and mitaki, are rich in special polysaccharide compounds with names like *lentinan* and the *peptidomannans* which research studies have shown to exert powerful immune-enhancing effects on the body, increasing the number of the body's natural killer cells and activating the production of interferon and other immune-boosting elements. Shiitake are an important element in the daily Japanese diet. They are now widely available in the West in oriental food stores and health-food stores and even in some supermarkets. You can buy them in dried form, soak them in water for half an hour and then use them in cooking or salad making. Extracts of one or more of the shiitake mushroom's immune-supporting polysaccharides (such as KS-2) are also available from healthfood stores. They can be helpful taken for a week or two at a time to help counter a viral illness.

Check out Cone Flower

Echinacea (*Echinacea angustifolia*) has remarkable properties to stimulate the immune system, heal wounds, enhance skin, counter infection, and calm inflammation. You can take it in capsule form, 1–4 capsules 3–4 times a day, depending on whether it is being used as a prophylactic or as a treatment for illness. In the form of fresh plant tincture it can be taken in a little water: 15–50 drops at a time once or twice a day for prevention; several times a day as treatment; up to 2 teaspoons an hour for a day or two at the onset of illness.

Echinacea is wonderful insurance against illness and premature ageing, will help protect from colds, 'flu and chronic fatigue and will boost immunity when illness strikes, as well as helping to slow skin degeneration.

Go for Gold

Golden seal (*Hydrastis canadensis*) has recently won scientific praise for its many benefits which include relieving nausea, calming digestive disturbances, banishing skin diseases and eliminating haemorrhoids. It is a potent nerve and endocrine gland tonic. It can be used as a douche in the treatment of vaginal infections, as a mouthwash in the treatment of gum problems, and can be used to fight off infections when they strike. It tastes very unpleasant so it is best to take it in capsule form: 1–4 capsules 3 times a day.

It is particularly good for soothing digestive upset and easing liver problems and to calm uterine contractions, but should not be used in pregnancy.

Adaptogens are Ace

When it comes to long-term energy support and enhancement there is nothing like using the adaptogens. Adaptogens are very special plants which began to be identified 40 years ago by Russian scientists looking for ways of preventing illness and increasing people's abilities to handle stress without doing damage to the body. Their effect on the body is non-specific, enabling them to increase a person's resistance to illness, help protect from damaging elements such as chemicals and internally-manufactured wastes as well as from lifestyle pressures such as overwork or too little sleep. Adaptogens, unlike any drugs, also tend to have an ability to normalize bodily functions. In other words, they can help lower blood pressure that is too high, yet raise blood pressure in people where it is too low. Finally, adaptogens are non-toxic and they cause minimal disruptions in a body's biochemical and physiological functioning.

Since the early Russian studies of adaptogenic plants, primarily Oriental and Siberian ginseng, many more have been identified, a good number of which have long played an important role in Chinese medicine. The best way to use any adaptogen is to take it for a period of a month, then stop for two weeks and begin again. (This is one of the principles of natural medicine: since the body tends to become accustomed to whatever it is given over a long period of time, its beneficial effect can be decreased. By opting for regular periods of 'rest' one can prevent this from happening and reap an adaptogen's greatest benefits as a result.)

Stress Buster

Oriental ginseng, grown in China, Korea and Japan, is probably the most studied plant of modern times. It has been praised for centuries for its rejuvenating properties, its ability to protect against illness, to enhance the body's ability to handle stress – even to prolong life. There are a couple of things to note about ginseng, however: that a lot of ginseng on the market is not very good; and that many of its effects will be lost if you take more than 2 grammes of vitamin C a day, whereas taking vitamin E will enhance its actions.

Ginseng helps to heighten immunity, improve the functions of heart and lungs, counter fatigue and balance female hormones. Always buy the best quality you can afford and take it either as a fresh root tincture (5–20 drops 1–3 times a day), as an infusion or as a tea in which 25g (1oz) of the dried root is taken in a cup of water each day, or by chewing on a piece of the root the size of the tip of your little finger every day. Ginseng's effects are cumulative so you will need to take it for 6 to 8 weeks to feel its full benefits. (See Resources, p. 149, for a good source.)

Amazon Power

The most exciting adaptogen I have come across for a long time is suma (*Pfaffia paniculata*). Locally known as *para todo* ('for everything'), suma has been used by Brazilian Indians for centuries as an aphrodisiac and general tonic. Recent research has discovered that, like

110

pure ginseng, the wild root of the suma plant has power to enhance energy and protect against fatigue and damage from stress.

Researchers have found that a major source of the plant's energy-enhancing and protective properties lie in its ability to detoxify connective tissue of what are called *homotoxins*. These are wastes which interfere with the active transport of nutrients to our cells and in the production of cellular energy, and lead in the long term to changes in DNA associated with premature ageing and the development of degenerative diseases. What all of this means to the energy-seeker is that suma is well worth looking at as a nutritional support to raise your energy levels, enhance your ability to be very active both mentally and physically without fatigue or damage, and detoxify your cells as a prevention against premature ageing, cellulite and overall degeneration.

Energy Healing

From the point of view of quantum physics and of many of the world's great systems of healing – from Indian Ayurvedic teaching to Chinese medicine and laying on of hands – human beings are energy fields. These fields are constantly expanding, contracting and changing as our thoughts, diet and lifestyle change. Yet energy is seldom taken into account by the designers of food supplements. There is one green supplement, however, that is a real energy knockout.

One of the most interesting researchers to look into the area of life force treatments for healing and regeneration is the American healer Mitchell May. At the age of 22 May was in a car accident that rendered him profoundly damaged. He lost several inches of bone from his legs, and the tissue and nerve damage was extensive. He lay in insufferable pain. His physicians told him he would never walk again and that it was necessary to have his right leg amputated. They also informed him that his immune system would be permanently compromised and that his health would be severely restricted for the rest of his life. May was lucky enough to have been hospitalized at one of the most important medical research centres in the world, the University of California Medical Centre at Los Angeles. There he became part of a special study involving ongoing experiments into life force healing and extra-sensory perception in which skilled spiritual healers worked under strict scientific controls. He met and worked with a gifted healer named Jack Gray, and working intensely with him over a period of years, May returned to full and vibrant health.

Energy Dragon

May set out to discover, test and record information about specific foods and plant compounds that can enhance human health – not only chemically by supplying an abundance of vitamins, minerals, phyto-antioxidants and immune-enhancers, but also by providing an abundance of life force. He wanted to find ways of making it possible to help people live at their fullest energy, vitality, and wholeness, in maximum health and wellbeing.

Twenty years of painstaking experimentation enabled May to identify certain organically grown foods and plants and to combine them in a carefully formulated, synergetic way, so that the energies of each balanced the energies of the others. Out of this he developed the most remarkable nutritional supplement called Pure Synergy. Its combination of 62 of nature's most potent and nourishing components include organically grown freeze-dried herbs, organically grown immune-supporting mushrooms, plant enzymes, freeze-dried royal jelly, wild crafted algae, organic green juices and many other natural ingredients, and is the finest green superfood so far made. (See Resources, p. 149.)

Energetic Rejuvenation

May and others like him such as David Peat and double Nobel nominee Robert O. Becker have delved deeply into the field of subtle energy. They are helping to build bridges between orthodox, chemically-based, allopathic medicine (which until recently paid little attention to the energetic aspects of healing) and the ancient traditions of medicine which have always viewed healing as primarily an energy art. It is time to review our patterns of materialistic thinking about the body which ignore or underestimate interactions between consciousness and biochemistry. Plants share their energy with us when we begin to listen to them and experiment with them. Choose one or two which you want to get to know better and use them. Record in your energy workbook how they 'speak' to you on an ongoing basis. Your energy levels will be glad you have.

Step Eight
Charge Your Batteries

Your body is a mass of atoms and molecules in constant motion. Their shifting and whirling creates clouds of electrons and organized masses of magnetic fields, starting at a sub-molecular level and going right on up to the level of your organs and glands and systems. An alive body – a body able to call on energy for thinking and feeling, movement and creativity – is a body in which heightened levels of electron transfer are commonplace and in which energies are highly ordered. Exercise helps you get your body that way and keep it that way. In a living human body, movement breeds energy. So does rest and relaxation as well as simple do-it-yourself energy tricks like using hot and cold water or experimenting with special breathing techniques. All of these things can be used to shift body energy in your favour. Let's look at exercise first.

Move into Energy

Energy for work and for your body's metabolic activities is produced in your muscle cells in little energy factories called *mitochondria*. Here it is stored in the form of *adenosine triphosphate* (ATP). When your body needs energy to carry out some task like breaking down a protein or producing a hormone or thinking a thought, it calls upon ATP in the mitochondria rather as you might go to your bank to withdraw cash from an account in order to pay a bill. When you exercise regularly for at least a six-month period important changes take place in your cells. The number of mitochondria in each cell increases. This creates more sites for the production of the energy-rich ATP so that the total quantity of this compound increases and it is produced much more rapidly than before. This is one of the reasons why people who take up a programme of aerobic exercise report they discover new reserves of vitality. An American professor of physical education, Tom Cureton, surveyed some 2,500 people who took up regular exercise and found that they had significantly more energy and less tension than when they led more sedentary lives. The physical, mental and spiritual rewards of exercise are so far-reaching that to say you *should* exercise because it lowers your cholesterol or firms your thighs sounds like a banal understatement. It could better be said that the right kind of regular exercise can transform your life.

Take It Easy

We in the West have this weird notion that if a little of something does you good, twice as much good will come from a double dose. When it comes to using physical activity to boost energy nothing could be further from the truth. For physical activity to create more energy in your life, the exercise you do has simply to be regular, consistent, rhythmic and to involve large muscle groups. It should also be carried out at about 70–85% of your maximum heart rate or MHR. Your MHR is easy to calculate:

Work out Your Maximum Heart Rate

Your target rate for physical activity is 70–85% of your maximum heart rate. Here is how to calculate your own MHR.

- Subtract your age from 220. For instance if you are 36 years old, your MHR would be 220 minus 36 or 184.
- Your ideal aerobic range is then calculated by multiplying that number by 0.7 for the low end and 0.85 for the high. For this 36-year-old that works out at 129 to 156 beats per minute.
- When you are exercising within this range it is considered safe.
- If you are exercising to help raise your self-esteem, get rid of depression and anxiety or encourage fat loss you need to exercise so your heart stays around the lower figure – 129.

How to Check Your Pulse

After a few minutes of exercising, stop and put three fingers over the radial artery at your wrist to find your heart beat. Using a watch with a second hand count the number of heart beats over a period of 15 seconds. Then multiply this by four and you will know immediately if you are working out in the right range.

Begin by choosing the right activity for you. If you love company then solitary jogging down a country lane may suit you less than joining a gym or taking a dance class with friends. If you are shy and easily discouraged by the idea of exercising in public you might be happiest working out with an exercise video in your home. For the beginner who wants to make exercise a regular habit, I have found three forms of exercise particularly helpful because they are so simple: walking, rebounding and running.

Whatever exercise you choose should fulfil the following criteria:

- It should be sustained and non-stop.
- It should last at least 30 minutes.
- It must keep your heart beating at about 70–85% of its maximum capacity during the whole time you are exercising. Exercising harder than this can lower energy levels, not raise them. If you want to get fitter faster, exercise longer rather than harder.
- It should be done at least four times a week.

Here are a few suggestions:

Three Paths to Energy

One: Walk Over Your Exercise Hang-Up

Ideal for anyone who thinks they are too unfit to exercise.

Although it may seem like a soft option, in fact walking is one of the very best forms of aerobic exercise. A six-mile

116

walk burns up only 20% fewer calories than a hard run over the same distance. An excellent choice for anyone who feels low in energy or who is convalescing, walking is also particularly convenient because you can incorporate it into your daily routine to get you from A to B.

To begin with decide to walk for half an hour a day at a pace where your breathing becomes heavy but not strained. Make sure you wear comfortable clothes and good walking shoes. If you walk to work you can carry another pair of shoes with you to change into. After a week of walking for half an hour a day, go a step further. Try walking for an hour and see how far you get. As a guideline you should be able to manage 3 miles in an hour at a leisurely pace or 3½ at a brisker one. As you become stronger you might like to try hill-walking or even graduate to running.

Two: Bounce into Shape
Rebounding is the perfect solution for anyone who wants to exercise at home, no matter what their fitness level.
Unlike many in-the-home exercise options, rebounding has a particularly high continued use success rate. In case you are unfamiliar with the term, it means bouncing up and down on a mini-trampoline. Apart from being fun in the most natural child-like way, rebounding has some extraordinary health benefits thanks to the forces of gravity exerted on you as you bounce. At the top of each bounce – for a split-second – gravity is non-existent. You experience weightlessness like an astronaut in space. At the bottom of a bounce, gravity is increased by two to three times its normal force. This rhythmic pressure on each of your body's cells stimulates the lymphatic system to eliminate stored wastes – the type of wastes which incidentally are responsible for cellulite. Rebounding is not only great for newcomers to exercise, but is also often used by athletes as part of their training programme – particularly to repair and rebuild muscles after an injury.

Begin bouncing gently so that your heels barely leave the ground. If you feel unsteady, use the back of a chair to support yourself with one arm as you bounce. You might like to bounce to music or even while watching your favourite television programme. As an alternative to bouncing with both feet together, try jogging from one foot to the other. Begin with ten to fifteen minutes a day and work up to half an hour or so as your strength increases. You can also do various exercises on the rebounder to work the muscles throughout your body.

Three: Run to Freedom

Ideal for anyone who is keen to experience the high-energy benefits of regular exercise quickly.

Running is perhaps the most adaptable and practical of all forms of exercise. For anyone who travels often it can

---

Plan Your Schedule

Make an exercise schedule for the coming week in your workbook. Ideally try to include at least three 30 minute sessions of your activity. Begin with 20 minutes and work up to 45 or more. Make time for your exercise by planning in advance.

Chart Your Present Co-ordinates

Getting fit, like getting anywhere, means knowing where you are setting out from. Check your pulse to work out your present fitness level and establish your ideal work-out range. Write this down. Be sure to exercise at this level for optimal rewards. In a month's time you can take your pulse again to mark your improvement, and to keep an eye on exercising within your ideal aerobic range.

Set Your Goal

Make a reasonable goal for yourself and write it under your schedule. Don't invite failure by being unrealistic. Your goal should be a challenge but not an impossibility. When you achieve your first goal, set yourself a new one.

Mark Your Progress

Keep an exercise log in your workbook to record your progress. Make a note of anything you notice in relation to your exercise session. Not only will this make you conscious of your progress but it will give you the courage and incentive to keep going when you encounter resistance.

---

be ideal. Running shoes, shorts, a T-shirt and running bra (plus a thin waterproof top and Walkman if you like) take up minimal space in a suitcase. You can also run almost any time and anywhere. Begin by making a circuit for yourself of about a mile. Start out slowly and jog as far as you can. Don't push yourself so hard that you are breathless. At the right pace you should still be able to carry on a conversation as you jog. If you do find you get out of breath, alternate running with walking. Above all be patient. After a week or two, see if you can run the whole mile. When this becomes easy, increase your distance until you can run 2 or 3 miles. If you are really ambitious you might like to try running a marathon. Experts claim that once you can run for 45 minutes you can begin to train for one.

Choose from one of the above or some other activity, then get out your energy workbook and do some planning in black and white.

Extra Help For Exercise

If you find you need extra incentive to get yourself moving you might try one or more of these.

- Find a picture of your chosen activity or an inspiring quotation (I like 'Just Do It' in big letters) and pin it up on your bathroom mirror, your refrigerator and your desk for encouragement.

- Before you go to bed at night, give yourself a pep talk about your activity the following day and envisage yourself enjoying it.

- Lay your exercise clothes out ready for the next day. Many runners agree that the hardest part of a morning run is putting their shoes on and stepping out of the door. After that it's easy.

- Make a deal with a good friend to get fit together. Sharing the challenge of reclaiming body power with a friend is much more fun. (It can also give you a chance to moan and sympathize over aches and pains.)

- If you choose walking or running as your activity, cajole, borrow or buy a dog to accompany you. Dogs seem to have endless enthusiasm for walks and runs (however bad the weather).

- Experiment with different kinds of exercise to find which you enjoy most. Enjoyment is an important factor in making exercise work for you.

- Make a note of how you feel on the days you don't take exercise as well as those on which you do, then compare them.

- Hunt for a good coach or teacher – especially if you choose to work out at a gym or take an exercise class. The right one can provide encouragement and motivation.

- Let yourself daydream about how your body will change for the better in the next few months – the imagination is a potent tool in your quest for more energy.

Just Do It

In the beginning most of us are resistant to exercise. We sometimes feel we have to kick-start ourselves into action and it's not easy. But just as soon as you start to experience some of the benefits of exercise, like having more energy and feeling great about yourself, they will help spur you on. If you continue long enough (and 'long enough' is different for everyone) one magical day you will find you are actually beginning to *enjoy* yourself. Then, instead of dreading the next exercise session and finding excuses not to do it, you look forward to it. Of course this does not make you immune to resistance – or excuses. You may still stop exercising for a period of time; we all do. But because you have experienced the fun of it and the tremendous boost in energy it gives you, sooner or later something will call you back. Returning to exercise will be easier each time.

Then Let Go

So much for dynamism. What about its opposite – relaxation and utter surrender to bliss? They are equally important to lasting energy. For energy to be sustained, dynamism must be balanced with gentle ease. 'What goes up must come down' as the saying goes. These few words should be engraved on everyone's brain – particularly those of us who opt for a high-energy lifestyle. To experience high energy in a healthy way – not by taking drugs, drinking coffee or burning yourself out with stress – you must be able to let go, and to do so completely at will. That is something that most of us have to learn. After all, urban, 'civilized' society is not the best possible environment for keeping in touch with life's natural rhythms. Yet learning to move with these rhythms is central to calming and clearing your mind, restoring energy and balancing the excitement of being on the go.

Make a Friend of Your Body

How often do you rejoice in your body? How often do you feel at ease in your skin, at peace with yourself and in harmony with your world? For most people the answer is seldom. We tend to *put up with* our bodies as though they were slightly cumbersome things we have to carry about with us. Yet all thought, all feeling, every response to beauty and to horror comes through your body. It is your medium for experiencing everything in life. As any healthy two-year-old can show you, when *it* is fully alive *you* are fully alive. Such aliveness is central to energy. Young children have it naturally. Most of us have to rediscover it.

121

Many of us only notice our body when it causes us pain or discomfort. We blame it when it lets us down through injury or sickness. We chastise it for not being the right shape or size. At best we ignore it. But how often do we approach our body with a sense of gratitude for supporting and protecting us? For translating our desires into actions? For allowing us to experience a myriad of feelings and sensations which bring meaning to our life? Here is the chance to make amends. Show your appreciation for your body, use it and nurture it.

Take out your energy workbook and make a list of all the things that bring pleasure to your body. Then commit yourself to enjoying one or more of these things within the next 3 days. See just how much enjoyment your body can take!

Here are a few of my favourites:

- Eating fresh lychees and mangoes
- Making love
- Running along the cliffs above the sea
- Smelling lilies and freesias
- Watching a good movie
- Being massaged
- Feeling the breeze on one's face on a motorbike ride
- Swimming naked
- Listening to music
- Lounging in front of an open fire
- Reading a good book
- Drinking superb red wine

What are yours? Write them down, then figure out how you can encourage them into your life.

Your Body Has Its Rhythms

Another valuable way to energize your body long term is to increase your awareness of your natural rest–work cycles. Begin listening to the needs of your body instead of telling it what to do. We all have different lengths of time over which we are able to sustain activity (both mental and physical) without losing interest or becoming fatigued. For most people these are much shorter than they think. It is often much easier to judge with a physical activity than a mental one because physical fatigue is more apparent. Yet mental and emotional efforts can be just as tiring as doing athletics or putting up shelves. Office workers and housewives are treated far more often for fatigue than labourers. If you want more energy become aware of when you are tired and get into the habit of resting rather than driving yourself even harder.

Listen to Your Body

The way to check for fatigue is to be aware of which part of your body shows signs of it first. It may be your shoulders, your back, or your eyes. Or it may show in irritability or lack of concentration. When the sign appears, heed it. Take a short rest or break. Even a five-minute break will help you return to your work with increased vigour and concentration. Tests have shown that people work far more productively when their work is interspersed with such breaks. Time spent on a break is more than made up for by the amount of time which will otherwise be wasted on unproductive thought and activity if the person is tired. If you continue to work when you are fatigued, the cells in some parts of your body may not be receiving the nutrients they need nor be eliminating their wastes properly. They remain, as you do, at a low energy level. A short rest allows the cells to get rid of their wastes and take in the nutrients they need to revitalize themselves.

The best kind of break you can take when you need one is to do something as different as possible from the activity you have been engaged in. If you've been working at a desk get up and walk around, run to the corner of the street and back, splash cold water on your face. If you have been doing something physical stop and sit still, breathe deeply or focus carefully on something in the room for half a minute.

A Breath of Energy

Working with your breath is another great way to get in touch with your body's energy rhythms. And little wonder, since the breath itself is a carrier of life energy. It is the energy of oxygen, without which none of the metabolic processes that create energy take place. Most of us, when under stress, shut down our capacity for full breathing. This means less oxygen gets to our cells and more carbon dioxide wastes are retained in them, all of which inhibits our ability to experience a high level of energy and to maintain balance. Anxiety, depression, a sense of meaninglessness, addictions and irrational fears are all telltale signs of a low breathing capacity. The poor breathing which most of us do leads to elemental deprivation where your cells and tissues are not only missing out on optimal levels of oxygen but on other vital elements such as boron and beryllium which are carried in minute quantities on the breath. Learning to breathe fully takes a bit of practice but it is a skill that is useful to relearn if you want to live at the peak of energy levels.

Breathe Free

Here's how. Even before you get out of bed in the morning take 30 breaths through your nose during which you are consciously aware of the air entering and leaving your body and of the way it interacts with your chest, belly, diaphragm and nasal passages. You don't have to *do* anything or change the rhythm of your breathing in any way. You simply need to be aware of what is going on in your body as you draw air into it and release air from it. Don't be surprised if at first this feels a bit awkward. As you practise this technique day by day over a period of several weeks you will find both that your energy levels

---

Breath Fix for Energy

It is actually possible to breathe in energy. Try this for a couple of minutes: close your eyes and breathe slowly and deeply, imagining that you are breathing in vitality from the air. As you breathe in, feel that your whole body is becoming more and more relaxed. Imagine it as a centre of light radiating outwards in all directions, as though you are taking in energy, transforming it into light and radiating it out again.

---

increase and that you experience a sense of balance in yourself. It takes no more than five or six minutes a day.

When you are low in energy you often think you should get more sleep. But is that right? And what if you can't? Sleep too is a great energy-balancer. It is also a fine healer. It regenerates your body, rejuvenates your face and helps restore the vitality you need to think and work at top efficiency – provided, of course, that you get enough of it. But how much sleep is enough? Some people get by quite well on five or six hours per night, while others require a full eight hours. The amount of sleep you need is an individual matter, so it is impossible to make hard and fast rules about it. The better your diet – the higher it is in fresh fruits and vegetables and natural, unprocessed foods – and the more exercise you get daily, the less time you are likely to need to sleep. What matters most is not the duration of your night's sleep, but rather its quality. If you don't sleep a lot, stop worrying about it. Use the time to read or write, to listen to music, to day-dream and play mind games.

Get into Water

One of my favourite energy-enhancing and energy-balancing techniques is the use of hot and cold water applications on the surface of the body. Using water in this way has the remarkable ability to energize you when you are down as well as calm you when you are over-stressed. I use it often and swear by it.

The use of hot and cold water – it is a practice known as contrast-hydrotherapy – can stimulate adrenal functions, alleviate inflammation, enhance hormone production, firm skin, balance the nervous system, strengthen muscles and energize the body and psyche. The greater the contrast between the temperature of the water applied to the skin and body temperature itself, the greater the effect contrast-hydro produces.

Using hydrotherapy for energy is easy provided, of course, you are generally healthy and not suffering from a heart condition. It is a simple matter of developing new habits. Hot water is applied to the whole body for three or four minutes in the form of a hot bath or shower, followed by thirty to sixty seconds of cold water. This procedure is repeated three times. The application of cold water need only be long enough to make the blood vessels constrict, and this has been shown to take place in as short a period as twenty seconds.

Contrast-hydro makes you feel great – but it is important to start slowly, increasing the length of your exposure to hot and cold water gradually. There are several ways you can do this. It can be done in the shower by taking a three-minute hot shower followed by twenty seconds to one minute of cold, repeating this three times beginning with hot and ending with cold. Alternatively, if you have a bath and shower which are separate you can use the bath for one temperature application, the shower for the other, getting in and out of each. During the summer make your bath cold and your shower hot. During the winter you can reverse this, making your bath hot and your shower cold.

Water World

There are some very important rules of hydrotherapy, for like any natural treatment it has to be followed carefully and wisely both to get benefits from it and to ensure that no harm is done to the body in the process.

Hot & Cold Protocols

- Always make sure that your body is warm before beginning any contrast-hydrotherapy.
- See that the room is well heated. At no time during hydrotherapy should the body become chilled.
- Always begin with a hot application and end with a cold.
- Begin slowly with 2–3 minutes of hot application followed by 20 seconds of cold. As your body accustoms itself to contrast-hydrotherapy you can increase the time of the cold application up to 1 minute.
- After water contrast-hydrotherapy dry your body well and make sure that you do not become chilled.
- Don't use contrast-hydrotherapy if you have any kind of organic disease, nervous disorder, high blood pressure, insulin-dependent diabetes, if you are very weak, or suffering from hardening of the arteries.
- Always check with your doctor before beginning any natural treatment to make sure that it is appropriate for you to use.

Exercise, relaxation, breathing techniques and water-works are all useful for energy-raising and energy-balancing. But like all the tools and techniques you can use to build your own high-energy lifestyle they are here only to serve you. None of them is essential and deciding not to make use of one or more of them should provoke no guilt or self-recrimination.

What you are likely to find is that, as your energies begin to rise as a result of changing your diet, detoxing your body, shifting your mental attitudes and living a more authentic life from your soul you will probably be drawn to experiment with one or more of these things. As you do, record your experience and reactions to your experiments in your energy workbook. This will help externalize and make clear your likes and dislikes. It can help you chart your progress and identify other areas of energy enhancement you might like to incorporate in your life. Meanwhile you will be learning to build better and better bridges between the core energy of your soul and its expression in the outside world. This is the most important thing of all in building energy that lasts and lasts.

Step Nine
Grin and Bear It

What goes 'ha, ha, bonk'?
Someone laughing their head off.

You can detox, eat well, exercise, boost yourself with herbs and green foods and breathe like a demon, but if you are not doing what you really want to do or having fun with it all then you are still not going to have anything like an abundance of energy.

Let Yourself Laugh

The close relationship between emotions and health has been investigated for many years. The scientific press has long been full of papers which show the way that negative emotions such as anger, resentment, fear and despair, are major factors in the development of serious illnesses such as cancer and coronary heart disease. We know, for instance, that direct pathways between mind and immunity exist via anatomical connections that link the brain directly to organs such as the spleen and the thymus gland. We also know that hormonal secretions induced by emotions and thought patterns create a second pathway between mind and body which is carried in the blood. And research carried out by eminent scientists such as Myrin Borysenko at the Harvard Medical School have demonstrated that excess adrenaline from high levels of stress can significantly depress the body's immune system. And you can't have energy without a properly functioning immune system.

Accentuate the Positive

Until fairly recently, however, most of the focus of mind-body research has been on the negative. Now many scientists are more interested in charting the biochemical changes brought about by positive emotions and encouraging their use as tools for health and healing. They have found that laughter, relaxation, meditation and hope not only produce beneficial changes, such as lowered heart rate and breathing, but they even improve the way your body responds to stress hormones and bring about a shift in your perception of potentially stressful situations so you can look on them as challenges rather than as insurmountable problems.

There have always been those who preached the power of mind to influence body. Only recently have researchers begun to draw scientific maps of *how* this happens. Most of the new knowledge comes out of a fascinating medical and biochemical discipline with an absurdly long name: *psychoneuroimmunology* – or PNI.

The Science of Bodymind

PNI is the scientific study of *bodymind*. Leading researchers in the PNI field, such as Dr G. F. Solomon at the University of California, have discovered that the human mind (which includes our conscious thoughts and unconscious impulses as well as our *superconscious* or transcendent mind and our emotions) is elaborately interwoven with every function of the body via nerve pathways and chemical messengers – the endorphins, neuropeptides and hormones. A hormonal–nerve relationship exists between your endocrine glands, via the pituitary (master gland regulating the actions of all others), the adrenals (which deal with stress) and the hypothalamus. It is called (wait for it) the *hypo-thalamic-pituitary-adrenal-axis* and it links your thoughts and emotions with physical responses. With each passing month more scientific maps of bodymind are being drawn. They show how what you think and feel powerfully influence the levels of vitality you experience, as well as how slowly or rapidly you age, and whether or not you resist infections. Such information is invaluable to the high-energy seeker.

Energy Tip
Seek out and spend time with people who make you laugh –
often.

Anatomy of an Illness

Back in the 1970s the prestigious *New England Journal of Medicine* published a major article by Norman Cousins called 'Anatomy of an Illness'. It had the distinction of being one of the very few papers in the journal's history to be written by a layman, and it became one of the most widely reprinted and discussed medical pieces of this century. The article was a record of Cousins' recovery from a crippling and supposedly irreversible disease – ankylosing spondylitis – which causes the connective tissue in the spine to disintegrate. It recorded how, after being told that he had only one chance in 500 of recovery, Cousins decided to take his treatment into his own hands. Being aware of recent research, which showed how negative emotions brought about destructive chemical changes in the body, Cousins asked himself the question. 'Could the converse also be true? Could *positive* emotions foster *positive* changes as well?'

Go to the Movies

The article, as well as a book by Cousins of the same name, described how he went about testing his hypothesis. He discharged himself from hospital, altered his diet, gathered together a pile of old *Candid Camera* and Marx Brothers films, and began to watch them. With the help of his doctor, he set out to explore the question. They did tests called sedimentation-rate readings just before, and a few hours after, each episode of laughter. Each

---

Patient: 'Doctor, Doctor, I feel like a pair of curtains.'
Doctor: 'Pull yourself together, Sir.'

---

time gradual changes were perceptible; they tended to hold, so that improvement became cumulative. The result of Cousins' experiments have made medical history. He emerged healed, with his enthusiasm for life renewed, and with the determination to share with others his simple yet potent tool – laughter. Cousins uses laughter not only literally but as a metaphor for the full range of positive emotions, including hope, faith, love, playfulness, determination, purpose and a will to live. He also stresses the power of a patient–doctor relationship based on humour and goodwill in the healing process.

> Look out for books which make you laugh. Keep a file of cartoons and magazine articles which you can share with friends. Have fun with them.

Take Two Jokes and Call Me in the Morning

Research psychiatrist William Fry, who has been investigating humour's effects on body energy for more than 30 years, discovered that three minutes of laughter a day is equal to 10 minutes of hard aerobic exercise. It benefits the heart, increases the consumption of oxygen, reduces muscle tension, pulse and blood pressure. Fry believes that laughter is a kind of blocking agent – a buffer helping to protect us from the damage that negative emotions can do to the body. The interest in laughter as a tool for healing and for maintaining a high level of energy and wellbeing has suddenly made a quantum leap. French doctor and laughter advocate Pierre Vachet is prone to describing at length all of its benefits – how it deepens breathing, expands blood vessels, heightens circulation (bringing more oxygen to the cells) increases the secretion of hormones beneficial to the body, speeds tissue healing and stabilizes bodily functions.

Laugh Your Way to Freedom

Professionals working with laughter are quick to point out that laughter is not just for the ill and infirm. It is for everybody. One of the best things about humour is that it breaks through the tendency of each of us to take ourselves and our values too seriously. It breaks down the roles we play and liberates the self locked within. It is our tendency to identify with our own self-created image, fears, beliefs and assumptions that takes us away from the joy which is *normal* for each of us. We all need to seek out and spend time with people who make us laugh and to rediscover the art of being silly – like a child.

Humour and laughter are essential in the over-serious world of health and fitness which can make you neurotic about what to eat and not to eat – a world which tends to measure health not as joyous energy and creativity but in terms of cholesterol levels, blood pressure and sedimentation rates.

> How many psychologists does it take to change a light-bulb?
> 15, but it's got to really want to change.

Are You an Optimist or a Pessimist?

Optimism or pessimism is not simply about whether your glass is half-full or half-empty. It is about how you explain things to yourself – your habitual ways of viewing your life, and a negative outlook will seditiously sap your energy and your passion for life. Pessimists tend to view the bad things that happen to them as permanent, whereas optimists view setbacks as temporary. For example: 'you never listen' versus 'you are not listening.' My son Jesse is an optimist – and has been so from a very young age. When someone was nasty to him he would not say 'that person hates me' he would say 'I think there is something wrong with so-and-so today.' In just the same way, good things are categorized differently by the optimist and the pessimist. The pessimist might think 'I did well today', the optimist 'I always do my best'.

Transmute Negativity

Hope may spring eternal in the human breast – but probably only for the optimist. However, any of us can learn to look at things in a more optimistic or positive light, often simply by being aware of all the negative thoughts that we are carrying around with us. Take your workbook and write some of yours down. They can be anything: 'I am too ugly to exercise,' 'I am too lazy to commit myself to a healthy way of eating,' 'I am too selfish to give up chocolate (which I love) even though I think I have low blood sugar problems.' Now try taking the optimistic view: 'I will look great once I have been exercising for a while,' 'If I try eating for energy for 10 days I will have so much more energy I won't want to go back to convenience foods,' 'It's not my fault that I love chocolate. If I deal with my blood sugar problems I can still enjoy it occasionally, and will probably enjoy it even more.'

Just as negative thinking is a learned response in each of us, so each of us can learn to think of ourselves and our lives in positive ways. Practised daily you will find your energy levels beginning to increase, and laughter coming much more easily.

How many men does it take to tile a bathroom?
Three – but you have to slice them thinly.

Depressed Immunity

PNI has discovered that the body's immune system, that bulwark of defence (and without a properly functioning immune system you can forget about energy), is undeniably affected by behavioural patterns which can lead either to improved or to decreased susceptibility to disease. In simple terms, the happier you are and the better you feel about yourself and your life, the less likely you are to fall prey to illness of whatever sort – from a common cold to a life-threatening disease. It may be time to lighten up.

> What's the difference between a Californian blonde and a supermarket trolley?
> A supermarket trolley has a mind of its own.

Laughter is great for energizing our lives, in no small part because it breaks through all our pretensions, assumptions and habits. It's soul food, it goes straight to the core, setting our creative juices in motion. There are lots of ways to use these creative juices, once they start to flow, to further energize your life and make of it whatever you want it to be. That is where mind games come in handy.

Get into Mind Games

You have a great friend in your unconscious mind. Once you learn how it functions you can begin drawing on its almost infinite power for healing, creativity, and energy. The unconscious works in a very different way from its conscious counterpart. The conscious mind is critical, focused, linear and rational. It can only deal with one thing at a time. The unconscious knows no such barriers. Psychologists and other researchers who have studied how our unconscious processes behave have discovered that the unconscious recognizes no space/time limits. It does not separate what it experiences as happening now with what it experienced from earlier times nor even from what may come into being in the future.

What's Real?

The unconscious also cannot differentiate between a *real* event and an imagined one. It is this characteristic which is such a nuisance when we are experiencing our own negative *shadows* from the past. You know the kind of thing. Say when you were a child you once fell off a high bed, hurting your head badly. The head is long healed but the *feeling* from the experience still rests somewhere in your unconscious so that every time you go into a bedroom where there is a high bed you feel uneasy.

That is the downside. This timelessness and inability to differentiate between what is imaginary and what is real in the unconscious mind has an upside too which makes it especially useful in helping you release energy.

Unlike the conscious mind, which measures every thought with which you present it against external reality, the unconscious measures what it is offered only by the *intensity* of the image or experience it evokes. How vivid is it? How much emotive power does it carry? These are the criteria your unconscious uses in deciding to move into action or not. And when you allow your unconscious mind to play upon an intense image often enough it can actually help bring what it is imagining into being.

Train Your Imagination

In recent years the capacity of the unconscious to bring about whatever you give it to imagine has been recognized and is now much used in sports. To improve performance coaches get their athletes to sit or lie down, shut their eyes and day-dream, imagining themselves, say, clearing the high jump set higher than ever before. It works so well in improving athletic performance that it has now become standard practice with Olympic athletes.

The key to making use of this superb imaginative power of the unconscious mind for building energy has two sides to it. Firstly, provide your unconscious with vibrant images of what you want to create – images it loves to play on, whether they be words, or visual pictures, or even vague longings. See yourself brimming with vitality, laughing, having fun, being free to do and be whatever you are. Whatever they are these need to be images you find exciting, pleasing, fun. Secondly, let your mind play with these images *often* while in a deeply relaxed state, *again and again*.

Image Experiments

You might like to practise this for 10 minutes a day on the train returning from work or just before going to sleep at night. Have fun with it. Record the experiences you have when you practise your own mind games in your energy workbook. Watch how the vividness of the images increases and notice how the fun and energy keep pace with it. This way, using repetition and evocative words, images and thoughts, your unconscious mind's ability to alter your life for the better appears almost unlimited. Imagine yourself with more energy, achieving all the goals you want to achieve with ease and simplicity, taking each step boldly and tirelessly. Playing with images like this will not only help free your energy, it can make it soar.

Step Ten
Dare to Be You

The core of a human being – that source of virtually boundless creative power as well as physical and psychic energy – will never be found by dissecting the human body. Nor can it be arrived at by analysing the human mind. Yet a sense of what I call living from the core or the soul, an experience of living – living truthfully to your own values – is something each of us experiences at certain times in our lives.

Although most of us only happen upon this experience accidentally, it can also be cultivated by pursuing actions which we enjoy or which make us feel good about ourselves and our lives. It can happen when we fall in love, when we feel happy because everything seems in harmony around us or when we feel pleased with ourselves, our children, or some accomplishment. In such moments everything seems to fit together, or feel right, and life has meaning. Such a sense is central to an experience of living with energy.

The techniques for building a high-energy lifestyle are only of lasting value if you value yourself and live your life on that assumption. That is why Step Ten on the energy workbook takes us full circle – back to working with ourselves.

Tuning into Core Energy

Psychologist Abraham Maslow, who spent his life studying not human pathology but rather human beings who lived their lives with great energy, creativity and joy – he called them *self-actualizers* – referred to the special moments in our lives as 'peak experiences'. After examining the experiences of thousands of high-energy, creative and happy people he came to the conclusion that these self-actualizers have certain things in common. They tend, for instance, to be the healthiest people in society, both mentally and physically. They tend to have a lot of values in common too, such as prizing simplicity, wholeness, effortlessness, truth, honesty, uniqueness, completeness and perfection – in fact the same values one might expect mystics to possess. They are, in effect, people who tend frequently to have peak experiences – moments of great happiness, rapture, ecstasy – in which life's conflicts are at least temporarily transcended or resolved. Other psychologists, anthropologists and philosophers have also described Maslow's self-actualizing person. Carl Rogers – perhaps most appropriately of all – refers to Maslow's self-actualizer as a 'fully functioning' person.

Out of this work there has emerged a whole new picture of what it is to be human. No longer do we see a human being the way Freud did – as a collection of repressed destructive urges, only barely restrained by learned moral constructs from destroying ourselves and others. Now we realize people as potentially autonomous human beings. We recognize that the destructive and self-defeating tendencies which we all have are far less indicative of the hidden truth of a person than they are the results of a frustration in the expression of what Maslow called the Self – or soul – of life itself. You can achieve boundless energy together with happiness and freedom from this frustration and from negative thought patterns and the behaviour they engender simply by letting your natural self-actualizing tendencies (which in most of us are still weak or dormant) develop. Until they grow we all regress into fear and frustration or laziness. Once they become stronger, your life becomes an ongoing process of energy release, growth, and unfolding of potential as well as, quite simply, much happier.

What Are Your Peak Experiences?

On a clean page in your energy workbook describe a moment or moments in your life where you felt a sense of 'living from your core' – a time when everything seemed to work for you, where you felt fulfilled and good about yourself. If you are not sure you understand the idea, simply describe a moment when you felt particularly happy. Remember the scene as vividly as possible and use as much detail as you can to recall your impressions. Use this description as a reference point from now on for how good you can feel and how wonderfully life can fit together. As you become more and more self-actualizing and come to live more and more from your soul, peak experiences become more frequent.

Create New Visions of You and Your Life

Now start to dream of what it will be like for you to have all the energy you ever need. Begin to play with a number of clear mental pictures of yourself as fit, well and looking great. But don't just consider the physical changes you would like to make. Get to know the person you aim to be and see yourself in this image. Record what you see, hope for, want to bring into being in your energy workbook and refer to it often when you feel unsure of your goals and direction. Here are some of the characteristics of high-energy self-actualizing to use as inspiration:

● *An exceptional ability to cope with change and to learn from it.* Most people have trouble with change. It is unsettling and frightening. It needn't be. It all depends on how you look at it. We all face fear with changes but the more you come to live from your core – to manifest your soul energy – the more you will tend to view change not as threatening but as a challenge to learn from and grow from, whether any particular change at face value appears to be 'good' or 'bad'. As far as failure is concerned, instead of being a source of fear, it can be viewed as something that shows how to deal with a similar situation in the future. After all, human beings *do* fail sometimes.

● *No great worry about saying 'No'.* Assertiveness, not aggression, plays a central role in creating energy. It implies a strong sense of your individual right to your values and opinions and a tendency to respect the rights of other people. You need to be able to say no to a food or drink you don't really want, a request from a lover or spouse, a demand from a child or a colleague. The best way to develop healthy assertiveness is simply to practise it. It feels a bit strange at first but the more you do the easier it becomes. Paradoxically only when you are positively assertive can you discover what real unselfishness is, because then what you give is what you *choose* to give, not what you feel *obliged* to give.

● *A well-conditioned body.* This not only brings you energy, it also helps you cope with stress better, look better and younger and strengthens your sense of self-reliance. It also shifts hormonal balance and brain chemistry making you highly resistant to depression and anxiety and highly prone to feeling good about yourself and your life. Top-level fitness leads to a freedom to achieve excellence in other non-physical areas of your life as well. It increases stamina, strength and flexibility not only physically but emotionally as well.

● *A marked absence of common minor ailments and troubles.* Most people believe that the Monday morning blues or the aches and pains in joints after the age of 40 are a normal part of living. But they take up little space when you have an abundance of energy. 'Normal' means moving with ease, and feeling pretty good about things day after day – sometimes feeling very good indeed – not because something stupendous has just happened but because when you are really fit and well that is the *normal* way to feel.

- *Laughter comes easily.* An ability to laugh at the absurd (including at yourself when appropriate) and a sense of fun are perhaps the most important of all the high-energy characteristics. Joy is health-giving. The most delightful sense of humour often parallels a strong sense of purpose in a person – another high-energy characteristic.

- *Integrity.* The more you become a self-actualizer, the more you set your own standards and live up to them. Your values become a source of strength and energy for you. You don't have to compromise them to achieve some temporary advantage. You can feel the truth, be who you really are and make your life work. Hard to believe? It's time to act.

Now Individualize Your Vision

Not all of these characteristics will appeal to everyone although they do tend to be pretty universal amongst the healthy people whose lives 'work' – Maslow's *self-actualizing* or Carl Rogers' *fully-functioning* people. Any of them which don't seem relevant to you, forget – for the moment. Take a closer look at those that do seem to have meaning. Maybe make a few notes in your workbook about how you feel about them. How much do they apply to you, say on a scale of one to ten?

Look again in a few weeks after working with some of the tools and techniques in this book. What may surprise you is that these tendencies become more characteristic of someone the more they make use of all the tools for high energy. Keep them in mind and identify with them as much as possible. In addition to the characteristics listed, add your own. Then, when you are relaxing, let your mind play upon some of these things. Keep track of the changes in your body, your vitality, in how you look and in your feelings as you go along. Are your goals changing or are they simply becoming clearer and more focused?

Plan Your Way

The best way to make a commitment to a high-energy lifestyle and stick to it is to *make a plan*. The better organized and more definite a plan you make for yourself, the more you will benefit from the material in this book. Such a plan should set out your commitments and clarify your intentions. A definite plan helps you to take seriously what you are doing. It can also be a source of considerable personal insight. It must also be flexible; it will change as you change. That is part of the excitement of self-actualization.

No matter where you are now in relation to where you want to be in terms of energy and self-actualization, remember that the journey which will take you there begins with small, single steps. Be patient and just keep working and playing with it.

Look Back Then Forward

Go back to the key questions you asked yourself in Step Two. Have a look at them again and see if your answers have changed in any way, or if you feel that you now have the answers to some questions you were unsure about. Look closely at your answer to 'What do you want?' Some wants are grandiose, others quite humble. Revise your wishes if they need revising; otherwise underline them in red to re-validate their importance to you. Start with a desire you believe is within your reach and set yourself the goal of achieving it. Make notes of things you have learned about energy from the book that might help you achieve it. Diet? Professional help? Exercise? Herbs? When you are well on the way to achieving that goal, choose another and do the same again, or if you like do as I do, making several related goals all at once and working with them. Doing this over and over will gradually allow you to come to know and trust your own power to make the life you want. Learning to set goals is really helpful. It is easier to achieve anything if you have a goal to reach.

Achieving a goal is also the biggest incentive to achieving the next one and the best reinforcement for sense of personal development and power. But be realistic; even big goals are made up of lots of little ones, so concentrate on achieving the achievable in a sensible time.

When it comes to more specific commitments, pick your goals and write them out in your journal in clear positive terms, and in the *present tense*. For instance, do not say 'I will never eat chocolate again,' say 'I am eating wonderful energy food today – a taste sensation of a salad for lunch made from beautiful vegetables.' Be very specific about what you want to gain from doing this. Exactly how do you want to feel? Why are you doing it?

Be as Specific as Possible

The more specific your preliminary plan, the better. Pick one of your goals. Often a very practical one is best to start with – say, becoming more physically fit, or learning better methods of stress control or losing weight. Having written it down, plan how to go about it – in your workbook. Ask yourself what techniques you might use to reach your goal. Here is an example: You might write, 'I'll begin an exercise programme of *rebounding* (see page 117) tomorrow,' (This commitment entails a corollary – that of organizing the buying of a rebounder today to be ready for tomorrow. If this doesn't seem possible, you'll have to postpone your intention until, say, next week when it is. If a rebounder is too expensive then you will have to alter your exercise plan to fit in with the possibilities, say by going swimming three times a week or beginning to jog or going for brisk walks instead.) Or, 'Tomorrow morning I will go through my cupboards and throw out all the junk foods. I can then make a list of the types of foods I want to look for when I go to the supermarket at the end of the week.' Or, 'I will find out about local suppliers of herbs and green supplements,' or 'On Thursday I will telephone some of the companies mentioned in Resources to get a list of their products, so that I am well informed.'

It usually works best to identify both the practical goals you want to work towards and at the same time to define the more spiritual ones and record them in your workbook. This way they will reinforce each other. Such a preliminary plan helps establish a good sense of direction and enables you to work out just what you have to do and what you have to learn in specific terms to reach your goals.

As you move on into energy, record your progress as well as any setbacks in your energy workbook. This continues the process of refining and focusing your goals and identifying values. Meanwhile your workbook becomes a great friend to support you, make you think more clearly, mirror your inner and outer worlds and walk the energy path with you all the way along.

When in Doubt, Act As If

There is a lot of power in this suggestion. Pretence, which many people look askance at and demean, is often the mother of genuine improvement. The dilettante whose main interest in painting comes from a desire to impress at parties can find one day, wandering through the National Gallery, that caught unawares between silly statements about the pictures before him he has been stung by the bee of real aesthetic experience. Many a genuine passion has begun with such pretence and turned into something life-transforming for the pretender in the end. By 'pretending' to be as strong, healthy, energetic and self-aware as you would like to be, you both raise your expectations and put yourself in the frame of mind that can help to bring these things about. In the last chapter we looked at what a powerful tool the mind can be. You can programme your subconscious to change your conscious life for the better. If you tell your subconscious that you have an abundance of energy, it will get on the grapevine and tell your conscious mind that you do, indeed, have an abundance of energy.

Ask Questions

Use your workbook to ask important questions and record your answers to them when they come. But ask positive questions instead of negative ones like 'Why do I have no energy?' How many times in the past have you asked yourself 'Why is this happening to me?' or 'Why am I always so thick'? Did you get answers to these questions? Did they make you feel good about yourself? Try a positive alternative – it works far better to empower you. Try, 'What can I do to make the situation I am in better?' For instance, instead of asking yourself why you don't have any energy, start asking yourself 'What action can I take to create more energy in my life?' You can alter other areas of your life in the same way; for example, 'What do I need to do to be happier?'

The Morning Practice

Try this practice for two weeks. It can help you make the great shift from negative to positive. Each morning, go to your workbook, ask yourself the following questions and put down your answers.

1. How are my *energy levels* this morning?
2. What am I *happy* about this morning?
3. What am I *excited* about this morning?
4. What am I *grateful* for this morning?
5. What can I *do today* to help me achieve my goals?

Then, each evening, take another look at these questions and your answers, then answer the following questions.

1. How *were* my energy levels today? What affected them?
2. What have I *learned* today?
3. What have I *done* to be proud of today?
4. What did I do towards *reaching my goal?*
   or Now that I have achieved this goal, what is my *next one?*

All of these simple ways of working with your energy workbook can constitute a tremendously powerful support to your energy journey. Play with them and see for yourself how helpful they can be.

When Things Go Slow

What should you do when you are feeling low and in need of a boost? The first answer is simple – rest. Rest is a great energizer. If you try to carry on for too long without it, you will deplete your long-term vitality. Here are some other useful things to look at, and some guidelines you might find helpful when you find yourself in an energy slump.

What is High Energy Like?

Living a high-energy lifestyle does not mean rushing around like a headless chicken or being busy all the time. Far from it. Your energy, like the year, will have its seasons. There are times when it will be dynamic and others when it will be soft and tender. Some days you will use it to be brilliant or do battle against an obstacle which appears in your way. Other days your energy rhythms will be asking you to surrender yourself more wholeheartedly than ever before to the beauty of a piece of music or the abandonment of making love. High energy simply means an ability to live fully, to give of your very best and to be open to all the good things life has to offer. Once you learn how to tap into the energy within yourself and how to balance your dynamic rhythms with your surrendering ones, energy will never again be something you have to worry about.

Each of us is born with different energy levels. Each of us needs to experience dynamism, relaxation and joy. Love is the key to releasing your innate soul energy. When you are doing something you love or are with someone you love, you tap energy resources better than at any other time. Learn to do what you love and then you will love what you do. Most important of all, learn to love yourself. You are worthy of love. That magnificent individual soul at your core is the source of all your beauty, creative power, and energy. Go for it!

Low Energy Check-List

Stop doing everything yourself.
Start delegating, both at work and at home, and whenever you can, get someone else to do what needs to be done.

Reach for the top but never struggle in vain.
Take a close look at your values. What really matters to you? You can't have everything. Make choices. Otherwise you could end up a workhorse who's ultimately not very good at anything.

Don't say yes to everything.
When something is asked of you, give yourself time to consider the request before you immediately agree. Is it something you can handle with relative ease? What are you going to have to lay aside to do it? What is it going to cost you in terms of time?

Forget the hero image.
You are only human. And you'd be surprised how much pleasure it can bring to other people when they feel they can do something for *you* for a change. Express your needs and many of them are likely to be satisfied. Lock them away behind the perfectly together superhuman image you protect and you go it alone.

Guard your time jealously.
Limit the time you spend on inessential things such as seeing people you don't really care about just because you feel it is expected of you. Cut back on the chores you feel you have to do. Do you *really* have to? Or could somebody else do them for you? Or could they remain undone for the sake of your peace of mind?

Sort your priorities.
Take a look at what is absolutely essential to your life and what is marginal. Write them down in your journal then make sure the time and effort you spend on each thing is in line with these priorities. Take an active role in deciding how you will spend your time and live your life. Don't just let it happen.

Create a routine.
From day to day you need to make sure you have time to relax and to take care of yourself and time to spend with the people you love. Recreation and having fun are as important as hard work, responsibility and success. Make sure you get the balance right.

Resources

More from Leslie Kenton
Leslie's audio tapes including 10 Steps to A New You and others, as
well as her videos including Ageless Ageing, Lean Revolution, 10 Day
De-Stress Plan, and Cellulite Revolution, can be ordered from QED
Recording Services Ltd, Lancaster Road, New Barnet, Hertfordshire
EN4 8AS. Telephone: 0181 441 7722. Fax 0181 441 0777.
Email: enquiry@qed-productions.com

If you want to know about Leslie's personal appearances, forthcoming
books, videos, workshops and projects please visit her website for the
latest information:
http://www.qed-productions.com/lesliekenton.htm
You can also write to her care of QED at the above address enclosing
a stamped, self-addressed A4 size envelope.

Addiction Help:
Alcoholics Anonymous (London Region), 11 Redcliffe Gardens, London
    SW10. Tel: 0171 352 3001
Co-Dependents Anonymous, Ashburnham Community Centre, 69
    Tetcott Road, London SW10. Tel: 0171 376 8191
Drinkline National Alcohol Helpline. Tel: 0345 320 202
Eating Disorders Association (telephone helpline): 01603 621 414
Gamblers Anonymous. Tel: 0171 384 3040
Narcotics Anonymous Helpline. Tel: 0171 730 0009
Smoking and eating addictions: Contact Gillian Riley at 23 Stanhope
    Gardens, London N6 5TT, 0181 3487407. Gillian's work is excellent
    in both areas – simply the best.

Anti-Oxidant Supplements:
BioGuard supplies a one-a-day maintenance intake of the major anti-
oxidant nutrients. Available from: BioCare, Lakeside, 180 Lifford Lane,
Kings Norton, Birmingham, West Midlands, B30 3NU. Tel: 0121 433
3727. Fax: 0121 433 8705.
    Solgar's Advanced Antioxidant Formula is also good. For local sup-
pliers contact: Solgar Vitamins Ltd, Solgar House, Aldbury, Tring,
Herts, HP23 5PT. Tel: 01442 890355. Fax: 01442 890366.
    Both of these products are available direct or by mail order from
The Nutri Centre, 7 Park Crescent, London W1N 3HE. Tel: 0171 436
5122. Fax: 0171 436 5171.

Digestive Enzymes: Good digestive enzymes from plant sources are
available from BioCare (see above). Polyzyme Forte is a very strong,
broad-spectrum digestive enzyme, Digestaid is excellent for more

general consumption, and Biocidin Forte, taken by those with low blood-sugar problems, is traditionally used to help maintain the balance of intestinal flora. Carbozyme aids the digestion of beans and pulses to prevent flatulence. They are available from BioCare, see above.

Food Allergy testing: Biolab Medical Unit, The Stone House, 9 Weymouth Street, London W1N 3FF. Tel: 0171 636 5905. Fax: 0171 580 3910. This unit is a referral centre for Nutritional Medicine Biolab and the best nutritional analysis laboratory in Europe. Patients can be referred by their GP or hospital consultant. Doctors can also contact the unit for advice on laboratory investigations and the correction of nutrient deficiencies or imbalances.

Ginseng: A good ginseng comes in the form of Jinlin Ginseng Tea, Jinlin Panax ginseng dried slices, ampoules and Jinlin whole root, available from health food stores. If you have difficulty finding it contact Alice Chiu, 4 Tring Close, Barkingside, Essex, IG2 7LQ. Tel: 0181 554 3838.

Green Supplements:
Pure Synergy: Simply the best nutritional supplement, available from Xynergy Health Products, Lower Elstead, Midhurst, West Sussex, GU29 0JT. Tel: 01730 813642. Fax: 01730 815109.

Lifestream Spirulina: a particularly pure form in tablet and powder form is available from Xynergy Health Products (see above).

Chlorella is available in capsule form from Solgar Vitamins Ltd, Solgar House, Aldbury, Tring, Herts, HP23 5PT. Tel: 01442 890355. Fax: 01442 890366.

Wheatgrass Juice in powdered form is available from: The Nutri Centre. On the lower ground floor of the Hale Clinic, The Nutri Centre has the finest selection of nutritional products under one roof in Britain. It is also able to supply homeopathic products, herbal, Ayurvedic and biochemical products, flower remedies, essential oils, skincare and dental products, and has an extensive selection of books. They also have an excellent selection of green supplements, all available through a good mail-order service. Nutri Centre, 7 Park Crescent, London W1N 3HE. Tel: 0171 436 5122. Fax: 0171 436 5171.

Herbals: Herbal tinctures and extracts are available by mail order from: Bioforce UK Ltd, 2 Brewster Place, Irvine, Ayrshire, KA11 5 DD. Tel: 01294 277344. Fax: 01294 277922.

An excellent supplier of tinctures, fluid extracts, loose dried herbs and the Schoenenberger plant juices is: Phyto Pharma-ceuticals Ltd, Park Works, Park Road, Mansfield, Woodhouse, Nottinghamshire, NG19 8EF. Tel: 01623 644334. Fax: 01623 657232. Minimum order £20.

Another good source, and a supplier of Pau d'Arco tea, is Herbal Supplies, 3 Burton Villas, Hove, Sussex, BN3 6FN. Freepost BR 1396, Hove Sussex BN3 6BR. Freefone: 0800 2986698. Fax: 01273 705120.

The Nutri Centre also have a good range of herbs, including

Guarana and Kava: Nutri Centre, 7 Park Crescent, London W1N 3HE. Tel: 0171 436 5122. Fax: 0171 436 5171. They have the most comprehensive range of nutritional supplements, herbals, books and tapes on health in the UK. Mail order.

Pure herbal products can be obtained from Bio-Health Ltd. They do a range of pure herbal products which are a natural adjunct to a considered diet and a holistic approach to staying well; they are not intended to supplement a poor diet. The Bio-Health 'Pure-Fil' additive-free range is made from specially selected fresh herbs which are then dried, powdered and encapsulated under strict quality control. Bio-Health Ltd also do a range of classic herbal medicines. Call for a product guide. Bio-Health Ltd, Braboenf House, 64 Portsmouth Road, Guildford, Surrey GU2 5DU. Tel: 01483 570813. Fax: 01483 457101.

Herb Teas: Some of my favourite blends include Cinnamon Rose, Orange Zinger, and Emperor's Choice by Celestial Seasonings: Warm & Spicy by Symmingtons; and Creamy Carob French Vanilla. Yogi Tea, by Golden Temple Products, is a strong spicy blend, perfect as a coffee replacement. Green tea is available from health food stores and Oriental supermarkets.

Iron Supplements: A highly absorbable organic iron compound suitable for people sensitive to iron supplementation, Iron EAP2 is available from BioCare, Lakeside, 180 Lifford Lane, Kings Norton, Birmingham, West Midlands, B30H 3NU. Tel: 0121 433 3727. Fax: 0121 433 8705.

Desiccated liver tablets and a wide range of other iron supplements are available from the Nutri Centre (see above).

Liver Powder is available from health food shops.

Floradix is a good plant-based iron supplement for vegetarians, available from good health food stores.

Tincture of nettle, or nettle in plant juice form, has traditionally been used to help anaemia. Available from: Phyto Pharmaceuticals Ltd, see above.

Liver Support: Three excellent lipotrophic formulas are available by mail order through the Nutri Centre (see above). They are:

Nutriwest's Lipotrophic Plus formula: and BioCare's Silymarin Plus, a lipotrophic formula with milk thistle (also available from BioCare (see above)).

Milk Thistle (Silymarin) is available from good herbal suppliers.

Living Foods Workshops: Naturopath Elaine Bruce, who has spent eighteen years working with living foods as a tool for healing and teaching how to make delicious recipes, offers an intensive training in her own approach to health and vitality, Introductory weekend course: How to set up a Living Food Kitchen – small groups, individual attention, high quality organic produce. Contact Elaine Bruce, Holmleigh, Gravel Hill, Ludlow, SY8 1QS. Tel: 01584 875308. Email: elaine@livingfoods.enta.net.

Marigold Swiss Vegetable Bouillon Powder: This instant broth powder based on vegetables and sea salt is the best. It comes in Vegan and organic form too. It is available from health-food stores or direct from Marigold Foods, Unit 10, St Pancras Commercial Centre, 63 Pratt Street, London NW1 0BY. Tel: 0171 267 7368.

Natural Progesterone Information Service: NPIS, Box 131, Etchingham, TN19 7ZN. For information on the multiple uses of this natural hormone for women's health from puberty to menopause, and also a list of books, tapes and videos available write to above address.

For information about natural treatments for women contact: Well Woman's International Network
La Brecque, Alderney, Channel Islands, GY9 3TJ, Great Britain. Residing outside UK – Telephone +44(0) 7000 835994. Fax +44(0) 7000 3299941. Residing in UK – Telephone 07000 835994. Fax 07000 3299941.
The Well Woman's International Network (WWIN) is an organisation for women to use as a network resource to make contact and stay in touch with natural health developments that can make a vital difference to enjoying life to the full – regardless of age. They offer information on natural supplements and natural progesterone products. Patron Dr John Lee. WWIN effects a personal import service. Full range of natural hormone products (inc Vegan) at discounted prices for its members, postal/email consultation with specialist doctors, quarterly forum/ newsletter. Membership to this worldwide Well Woman's International Network is £30 (Sterling) per annum.

Progesterone Body Creams & Oils (in alphabetical order)
Dr John Lee states clearly that natural progesterone oils and creams which contain less than 800 milligrams per 2 ounce jar will not supply sufficient progesterone if you are truly deficient.

The following list of American products meet this criteria.

PROGEST – E Complex	Kenogen	Eugene, OR
Creams/Oils Containing 400–500 mg of Progesterone per Ounce		
Angel Care	Angel Care, USA	Atlanta, GA
Bio Balance	Elan Care, USA	Scottsdale, AZ
Edenn Cream	SNM	Norcross, GA
E'Pro & Estrol Balance	Sarati International	Pasadena, TX
Equillibrium	Equillibrium Lab	Boca Raton, FL
Fair Lady	Village Market	Fond du Lac, WI
Femarone – 17	Wise Essentials	Minneapolis, MN
Feminique	Country Life	Hauppage, NY
Happy PMS	HM Enterprises, Inc	Norcross, GA
Kokoro Balance Cream	Kororo, LLC	Laguna Niguel, CA
Marpe's Wild Yam	Green Pastures	Flat Rock, NC
NatraGest	Broadmore Labs, Inc	Ventura, CA
Natural Balance	South Market Service	Atlanta, GA
Natural Woman	Products of Nature	Ridgefield, CN
OstaDerm	Bezwecken	Beaverton, OR
PhytoGest	Karuna Corp	Novato, CR

Pro-Alo	Health Watchers Sys	Scottsdale, AZ
ProBalance	Springboard	Monterey, CA
Pro-G	TriMedica	Scottsdale, AZ
Progressence	Young Living	Payson, UT
Pro-Gest	Prof. Tech Serv Inc	Portland, OR
Progonol	Bezwecken	Beacerton, OR
Renewed Balance	America Image Marketing	Nampa. ID
Serenity	Health & Science Nutrition	n.Lauderdale, FL

You can purchase Progest by post from:
Woman's International Pharmacy
5708 Monova Drive, Madison W1, USA
Tel: 001 608 221 7800. Fax: 001 608 221 7819.

Nutritional Practitioners: For a copy of the CNEAT (Council for Nutrition education and Therapy) Directory of Practitioners – comprehensive list of practising nutrition counsellors – contact The Institute for Optimum Nutrition, Blades Court, Deodar Road, London SW15 2NU. Tel: 0181 877 9993. Fax: 0181 877 9980. Cost £2.50 including postage.

Nutritional Supplements:
Higher Nature Ltd, The Nutrition Centre, Burwash Common, East Sussex, TN19 7LX. Tel: 01435 882880. Fax. 01435 883720.
Higher Nature Ltd offers exceptional nutritional products – high potency vitamins, minerals, herbal tonics and superfoods. Optimum Nutrition, Essential Balance, Mexican Yam, Aloe Gold, Essiac, Flax Seed oil, Glutamine, Criticidal, Brain Food, Cats Claw, Sambucol, and Phosphytidyl Serine are some of the current bestsellers. Higher Nature are the distributors for the Natural Progesterone Cream, ProGest. Higher Nature offer the best allergy testing plus saliva testing kits available. The IgG ELISA Food Intolerance testing from Immuno Laboratories is renowned for its high level of accuracy. They are the world's leading laboratory for food allergy testing. Contact 01435 882880 for further details.

Revital Health Shop:
3a Colonnades, 123/151 Buckingham Palace Road,
London, SW1V 9RZ. Tel: 0800 252875 mail order
Revital supply natural health products such as food supplements, sports, fitness and diet, skin care, bodycare and aromatherapy, alternative therapies. Please telephone for mail order catalogue.

Organic Foods: Organic Direct, 1–7 Willow Street, London, EC2A 4BH. Tel: 0171 7292828. Organics Direct specialise in home delivery of organic, healthy food, free from pesticides and chemical fertiliser. Your order will be delivered anywhere in mainland UK within 24 hours, direct from the farm. They also do soup wine, beer, cider, juices, baby food. Please call the above number for a free catalogue.

The Soil Association publishers a regularly updated National Directory of Farm Shops and Box Schemes which costs £3, including postage, from The Organic Food & Farming Centre, 86 Colston Street, Bristol, BS1 5BB.

Organic Meat: Good quality organic beef, pork, bacon, lamb, chicken, a variety of types of sausage, and a selection of cheeses, can be ordered from Eastbrook Farm Organic Meats, Bishopstone, Swindon, Wiltshire, SN6 8PW. Tel: 01793 790460. Fax: 01793 791239. All goods are sent for next day delivery, vacuum packed and chilled.

Longwood Farm Organic Meats, Tudenham St Mary, Bury St Edmunds, Suffolk. IP28 6TB. Tel: 01638 717120. They also deliver a full range of other organic foods.

Pure Synergy: See Green Supplemnets.

Sea Plants: Sea plants such as kelp, dulse, nori, kombu and wakami can be bought from Japanese grocers or macrobiotic health food shops.

Shiitake & Maitake Mushrooms: These are available from Japanese grocers or macrobiotic health food shops. Shi-Ta-Ke Extract in capsule form is available from BioCare (see above).

Thyroid: Armour Thyroid is available from Forest Pharmaceuticals, Barnes Foundation, Trumple, CN, USA. Tel: 001 314 569 3610.

For further information about natural health and healing, women's reproductive health, detoxification, juicing, and the effect of environmental pollutants see:

The New Raw Energy Leslie and Sussannah Kenton, Vermilion, 1994. This meticulously researched book shows how fresh, uncooked foods can work wonders for your body and your life.

Raw Energy Recipes Leslie and Sussannah Kenton, Ebury Press, 1994. Eating lots of fresh, raw foods can help you look and feel younger, and protect against colds, 'flu, fatigue and stress.

Raw Energy Food Combining Diet Leslie Kenton, Ebury Press, 1996. Food combining is a smart way to shed unwanted fat without counting a calorie and it will make you feel more alive.

The New Biogenic Diet Leslie Kenton, Vermilion, 1995. Health, nutrition and permanent weight loss based on natural fresh foods that have been carefully combined.

10 Day Clean Up Plan Leslie Kenton, Ebury Press, 1994. A step-by-step guide to regenerating your energy while transforming the way you look and feel – all in ten days.

Juice High Leslie Kenton with Russell Cronin, Ebury Press, 1996. Discover how raw fruit and vegetable juices can energize your life, rejuvenate your body, expand your mind and free your spirit.

Passage to Power Because we are told so little, few women in our culture are prepared for menopause, nor for the next phase of their life. Exploring the biochemistry and physiology of menopause, alongside myth and archetype, this book will permanently transform the lives of women over 35.

Further Reading

Bodymind

Psychoneuroimmunology, Robert Ader, Academic Press, New York, 1981.

The Mind Body Effect: How Behavioral Medicine Can Show You the Way to Better Health, Herbert Benson, Simon & Schuster, New York, 1979.

Minding the Body, Mending the Mind, Joan Borysenko, Addison-Wesley, Reading, MA., 1987.

Anatomy of an Illness as Perceived by the Patient, Norman Cousins, Bantam Books, New York, 1981.

Laugh With Health, Manfred Koch, Henry Holt, New York, 1984.

Mind as Healer Mind as Slayer, Kenneth Pelletier, Delta Books, New York, 1977.

Getting Well Again, Carl O. Simonton, Bantam Books, New York, 1980.

Healing Yourself: A Step-By-Step Program for Better Health Through Imagery, Martin L. Rossman, Pocket Books, New York, 1989.

Candida albicans

The Yeast Connection, William Crook, Professional Books/ Future Health, TE, 1989.

The Candidiasis Syndrome, Old Problem, New Mystery, Keith Sehnert, U.A.S. Laboratories, Minneapolis, MN., 1986.

The Missing Diagnosis, C. Orian Truss, 3rd ed. Missing Diagnosis, Birmingham, AL., 1986.

Energy Health

The Body Electric: Electromagnetism and the Foundation of Life, Robert O. Becker and Gary Selden, William Morrow & Co, New York, 1987.

Your Vitality Quotient, Richard Earle, PhD & David Imrie, MD with Rich Archbold, Warner Books, New York, 1989.

'Healing Ourselves and Healing Our Planet' in *New Holistic Health Handbook: Living Well in a New Age*, Robert Muller, edited by Shepherd Bliss, Stephen Greene Press, Lexington, MA., 1985.

The Well Adult: Complete Guide to Protecting and Improving Your Health, Mike Samuels and Nancy Samuels, Summit Books, New York, 1988.

Food Allergies

Brain Allergies, William H. Philpott and Dwight K. Kalita, Keats Publishing, New Canaan, CT., 1987.

An Alternative Approach to Allergies: The New Field of Clinical Ecology Unravels the Environmental Causes of Mental and Physical Ills. Theron G. Randolph and Ralph W. Moss, rev. ed., Perennial Library, New York, 1990.

The Management of Clinical Allergy. Herbert J. Rinkel, Russell I. Williams, MD, Cheyenne, WI., 1983.

Herbs

The Holistic Herbal, David Hoffman, Findhorn Press, Findhorn, Moray, Scotland, 1983.

Herbs and Things: Jeanne Rose's Herbal, Jeanne Rose, Grossett and Dunlap, New York, 1972.

Way of Herbs, Michael Tierra, Pocket Books, New York, 1983.

Hypothyroidism

Hypothyroidism. The Unsuspected Illness, Broda Barnes, Harper & Row, New York, 1975.

Nutrition

Nutritional Self-Defense: Protecting Yourself from Yourself, Francis Sheridan Goulart, Scarborough House, Chelsea, MI., 1990.

Staying Healthy with Nutrition, Elson M. Haas, MD, Celestial Arts, Berkeley, CA., 1992.

Basic Natural Nutrition, John Heinenman, et al. Woodland Books, Provo, UT., 1984.

Ten Talents Vegetarian Natural Foods Cookbook, Frank J. Hurd and Rosalie J. Hurd, rev. ed., Ten Talents, Chisholm, MN., 1985.

Nutrition Almanac, John D. Kirschmann and Lavon J. Dunne, 2nd ed, McGraw-Hill Book Co, New York, 1985.

Mental and Elemental Nutrients: A Physician's Guide to Nutrition and Health Care, Carl C. Pfeiffer, Keats Publishing, New Canaan, CT., 1976.

The Healing Nutrients Within: Facts, Findings and New Research on Amino Acids, Carl C. Pfeiffer and Eric R. Braverman, Keats Publishing, New Canaan, CT., 1987.

Understanding Vitamins and Minerals, Prevention Magazine Editors, Prevention Total Health System Series, Rodale Press, Emmaus, PA., 1984.

The Complete Book of Minerals for Health, J. I. Rodale and Staff, Rodale Press, Emmaus, PA., 1981.

The Complete Book of Vitamins, Rodale Press Editors, Rodale Press, Emmaus, PA., 1984.

The Complete Book of Natural Foods, Fred Rohe, Shambhala Books, Boulder, CO., 1983.

Trace Elements and Man, Henry A. Schroeder, Devin-Adair, Greenwich, CT., 1973.

Nutritional Influences on Illness: A Sourcebook of Clinical Research, Melvyn Werbach, Third Line Press, Tarzana, CA., 1987.

Basic Nutrition and Diet Therapy Su Rodwell Williams, 8th ed. Mosby Yearbook, St Louis, MO., 1988.

Pollution

Household Pollutant Guide, Centre for Science in the Public Interest, Anchor Books, New York, 1978.

Nontoxic and Natural: How to Avoid Dangerous Everyday Products and Buy or Make Safe Ones, Debra Lynn Dadd, Jeremy P. Tarcher, Los Angeles, 1984.

Nontoxic Home: Protecting Yourself and Your Family from Everyday Toxics and Health Hazards, Debra Lynn Dadd, edited by Janice Gallagher, Jeremy P. Tarcher, Los Angeles, 1986.

Healthy Water for a Longer Life: A Nutritionist Looks at Drinking Water, Martin Fox, Healthy Water Research, Portsmouth, NH., 1986.

Passage to Power, Leslie Kenton, Ebury Press, Random House, London, 1995.

Troubled Water: The Poisoning of America's Drinking Water, Jonathan King, Rodale Press, Emmaus, PA., 1985.

Office Hazards: How Your Job Can Make You Sick, Joel Makower, Tilden Press, Washington, DC., 1981.

How to Survive Modern Technology, Charles McGee, Keats Publishing, New Canaan, CT., 1981.

Raw Foods

Food Enzymes for Health and Longevity, Edward Howell, Lotus Light Publications, Wilmot, WI., 1981.

Enzyme Nutrition by Edward Howell, Avery Publishing Group, Garden City Park, New York, 1985.

The Essene Gospel of Peace, Edmund Bordeaux Szekely, Book 1, Academy Books, San Diego, CA., 1977.

Index

adaptogens, 109–11
addictions, 35–40, 50
adenosine triphosphate
    (ATP), 114–15
adrenaline, 128
alcohol, 32, 106
algae, 105–6
allergies, 38, 41, 62–5, 72, 87–8
anaemia, 66–7
anger, 40, 41–2, 43
anti-depressant drugs, 43–4,
    46–7
anti-oxidants, 31
anxiety, 41
apples, 76
    apple raspberry frappé, 89
    live apple sauce, 89
apricot frappé, 89
assertiveness, 140
avocado and tomato soup, 93

beansprouts, 97
Becker, Robert O., 14, 113
blood sugar levels, 49–50,
    51–4, 71
body: attitudes to, 121–2
    listening to, 123–4
bodymind, 129
bouncing, 117–18
Brazilian cocoa, 107
breakfast, 84, 88–90
breathing, 124–5
bromelin, 76

caffeine, 71, 106, 107
Candida albicans, 29, 57–61

carbohydrates, 49–52
cashew nuts: nut mayonnaise,
    93
cereal grasses, 102–3
chicken, baked leeks and, 96
chlorella, 105–6
chlorophyll, 102, 103–4, 106
chromium, 50, 54
Chronic Fatigue Syndrome, 29
coffee, 71
colas, 71
compromises, 45
contrast-hydrotherapy, 126–7
convenience foods, 39, 43, 49,
    63, 68–74, 80
corn soup, 94
courgettes: sesame and cour-
    gette stir-fry, 95
Cousins, Norman, 130–1
crash diets, 40
cravings, 62, 65, 71–2, 87–8
cucumber soup, chilled, 94

dehydration, 70
depression, 43–8
detoxification, 16, 74–8
Devil's Delight, 91
dieting, 40
digestion, 80–1, 86, 87
dinner recipes, 94–6
dopamine, 46–7
dressings, 92–3
drugs, 60

eating out, 98–9
echinacea, 108

157

electromagnetism, 14–15, 34
electron transfer, 14, 114
elimination diet, 63–4
emotions, 40–1, 43, 44–5,
        128–31
energy, ten steps to, 15–17
energy-drainers, 12, 28–48
    addictions, 35–9
    depression, 43–4
    environmental pollutants,
        28–32
    food, 49–67
    heavy metals, 33
    lifestyle, 35, 39–40
    light, 33
    negative emotions, 40–5
    weather, 32
energy-enhancers, 12–13
enzymes, 63, 65, 84
Epstein Barr virus, 29
exercise, 31, 40, 74, 86,
        114–21

fasting, 74–8
fats, 72
fears, 42, 45
folic acid, 67
food: allergies, 38, 41, 62–5,
        72, 87–8
    and candida, 60, 61
    convenience foods, 39, 43,
        49, 63, 68–74, 80
    cravings, 62, 65, 71–2,
        87–8
    digestion, 80–1, 86, 87
    energy-drainers, 49–67
    fruit fasting, 74–8
    green foods, 102–13
    overeating, 39, 70
    raw food, 82, 88–99
food combining, 81, 82, 83–7
food sensitivities, 60, 62–5,
        87–8

fruit, 60, 82, 84–5, 88–9
fruit fasting, 74–8
full-spectrum light, 33

GABA (gamma-aminobuteric
        acid), 46
ginseng, 47, 109, 110
glucose, 50, 51, 52
goals, 142–4
golden seal, 108–9
grapefruit seed extract, 61
grapes, 76
grasses, 102–3
green foods, 90, 102–13
Green Glory, 91
green tea, 106–7
guarana, 107

healing, 111–13
heart rate, 115–16
heavy metals, 33, 34
homotoxins, 111
hormones, 54–5, 128, 129
hummus, raw, 93
hydrotherapy, 126–7
hypoglycaemia, 49–50, 51–4
hypothyroidism, 54–6

imagination, 135–6
immune system: Candida
        albicans, 57–8
    food allergies, 62, 63
    laughter and, 128
    liver and, 29
    psychoneuroimmunology,
        133–4
    supporting, 107–9
    toxins and, 28
inner voice, 24–5
insulin, 51, 52–3
involvement, 11
ions, 32
iron, 66–7

Jerusalem artichoke salad, 91
juices, 97
junk food, 68–74, 80

Kava, 47–8

lapachol, 60
laughter, 128, 129, 130–2, 134, 141
leaky gut syndrome, 63
leeks and chicken, baked, 96
life, 13–14
lifestyle energy-drainers, 35, 39–40
light, 33
limbic system, 47
lipotrophic agents, 31
listening to your body, 123–4
liver: detoxification, 29–32, 84
  as source of iron, 66–7
love, 146–7
lunches, 94–6, 98–9

mangetout and almond stir-fry, 95
mangoes, 77
Maslow, Abraham, 137–8, 141
Maximum Heart Rate (MHR), 115
May, Mitchell, 111–13
mayonnaise, nut, 93
melatonin, 33
metabolism, 16, 55, 56, 87
milk thistle, 31
mind, unconscious, 134–6, 144–5
minerals, 68, 104, 105, 106
mitochondria, 114

negative emotions, 40–1
negative thinking, 133, 135
noradrenaline, 47
nut mayonnaise, 93
nuts, 97

office pollution, 33, 35
optimism, 132–3
overeating, 39, 70
oxygen, 124, 131

pancreas, 51, 52, 72
papain, 77
papaya, 77
  Tropical Delight, 89
Pau d'Arco, 60
peak experiences, 138, 139
pear supreme, 89
pectin, 76
pessimism, 132–3
pineapple, 76
planning, 142–4
plants, green foods, 102–13
polenta, 96
pollution, 9, 28–9, 30, 33–5, 80
polyphenols, 106–7
potassium, 75
pretence, 144
probiotics, 61
protein, 80, 81, 84
psychoneuroimmunology (PNI), 129, 133
pulse rate, 116
Pure Synergy, 112

raw food, 82, 88–99
rebounding, 117–18
relaxation, 121
resentment, 40, 41–2, 45
rest, 123–4, 146
restaurants, 98
Rogers, Carl, 138, 141
Root-is-Best Salad, 92
Rowe, Dr Albert, 62
running, 118–19, 120

St John's Wort, 46–7
salads, 85, 90–2

salmon: green salmon stir-fry, 95
sea vegetables, 97, 104–5
Seasonal Affective Disorder (SAD), 33
seeds, 97
self-actualization, 137–42
self-esteem, 45
self-monitoring, 18–19
semiconduction, 14
sesame and courgette stir-fry, 95
shiitake mushrooms, 107–8
shish kebab, spicy, 95–6
Siberian ginseng, 47, 109
sleep, 19, 125
snacks, 73, 85, 94
soft drinks, 71
soul, 23–4, 137, 138
soups, 93–4
spirulina, 105
sprouts, 97
staple foods, 85
starches, 80, 81, 84
stir-fries, 94–5
stress, 128
subconscious mind, 134–6, 144–5
sugar, 50–4
suma, 110–11
Szent-Györgyi, Albert, 13–14

tannic acid, 71
tea, 71, 106–7

thrush, 57
thyroid problems, 54–6
tofu: pink tofu dressing, 93
toxins, 8–9, 28–30, 68, 87–8
trace elements, 104–5
travelling, 98
tropical delight, 89
truth telling, 23

ultra-high stir-fry, 95
ultraviolet (UV) light, 33
unconscious mind, 134–6, 144–5

vegetables, 60, 82, 90–2
vitamins, 68, 106
vitamin B12, 67
vitamin C, 67

walking, 116–17, 120
waste products, 8–9, 28, 68, 75, 87–8
water: drinking, 70, 86
  'high-water' foods, 82, 85
  hydrotherapy, 125–7
watercress salad, 92
watermelon, 77
weather, 32, 34
weeds, 104
weight gain, 69, 87, 88
winds, 32, 34
workbooks, 18, 78–9, 145–6

yeasts, 57–61